W9-CPB-851

PRAISE FOR *In Our Own Way*

"The very notion of preparing for life suggests developing mentally, physically, and spiritually. Boys of every color and culture have camped, learned, served, and prayed together as Boy Scouts. Dr. Edmonds has made an important contribution to those enduring pursuits as boys grow to become men."

—Reverend Michael E. Livingston
President, 2006–2007, National Council of Churches USA,
Executive Director, International Council of Community Churches

---

"*In Our Own Way* is a powerful reminder that our Scouting youth represent a rich tapestry of religious, ethnic, and cultural diversity in our country. Prayerfully, our youth of today will emerge as the leaders of tomorrow emboldened to uphold an authentic respect for the uniqueness that is Holy as understood by people of other faith traditions. Congratulations to Dr. Edmonds for his contribution toward helping to make that so!"

—Reverend Dr. Gwynne Guibord
Officer of Ecumenical and Interfaith Concerns, the Episcopal Diocese of Los Angeles, California, Consultant for Interfaith Relations, Office of Ecumenical and Interfaith Relations, the Episcopal Church

---

"*In Our Own Way* is a phenomenal expression of ecumenism through the sharing of prayers in differing faiths. The uniqueness of each faith's prayers shows the mutual benefit and blessing of praying together and for each other in one's own faith traditions."

—Reverend Dr. Daryl B. Ingram
Secretary-Treasurer, Christian Education, African Methodist Episcopal Church

"In Our Own Way is an inspiration. Not only can boys and young men find solace and words of faith and hope from their own tradition in these pages, but they can learn much about themselves in what their friends believe as well. This book is in the best tradition of Scouting and the best tradition of America. I recommend it highly!"

—RABBI GARY GREENEBAUM
U.S. Director of the Department for Interreligious Affairs, the American Jewish Committee

---

"In Our Own Way is not just a book on prayer; it is also a book of praying. The former instructs; the latter inspires. The passion and power of praying in Dr. Edmonds's book will deeply touch readers young and old from all walks of life."

—REVEREND DR. TONY RICHIE
Pentecostal representative in ecumenical and interfaith dialogue and Member, Commission of the Churches on International Affairs of the World Council of Churches, Geneva, Switzerland, Liaison for the Society for Pentecostal Studies to the Interfaith Relations Commission, National Council of Churches USA, New York, New York, Senior Pastor, New Harvest Church of God, Knoxville, Tennessee

---

"In Our Own Way is an amazingly comprehensive collection of prayers from major religions around the world skillfully arranged to meet the needs of Scouts and Scouting units."

—MARK HAZLEWOOD
Executive Director, Programs of Religious Activities with Youth (P.R.A.Y.)

"I am impressed with what Dr. Edmonds has put together for Scouts and Scouting."

—BRADLEY D. HARRIS
Associate Professor, Recreational Management and Youth Leadership, Brigham Young University

"What a wonderful work! This collection of prayers from various faith traditions will be of great benefit to those who seek the roots of Scouting in the divine virtues. All religions seek the face of God. This book helps us to see how Scouts from a variety of religious beliefs seek to be illumined by the light that shines on us from His face!"

—MONSIGNOR JAMES PATRICK MORONEY
Executive Director, Secretariat for the Liturgy, United States Conference of Catholic Bishops

---

"What we pray indicates what we believe. Here is a great resource of prayers and praying. *In Our Own Way* will be useful to individuals and groups searching for the words to use. Yet it is also more: it is helpful as an instrument of teaching and formation."

—REVEREND W. DOUGLAS MILLS, PH.D.
Associate General Secretary for Dialogue and Interfaith Relations, General Commission on Christian Unity and Interreligious Concerns, the United Methodist Church

---

"The message of *In Our Own Way* is meaningful to me personally. As the daughter of a dedicated Scout in Kashmir, I have seen firsthand how Scouts embody their belief that by serving humanity, you are serving God. With their sheer dedication to uplifting all people, Scouts have truly created a more peaceful and tranquil world. *In Our Own Way* exemplifies the Scouting ideals of self-sacrifice and service for all people. It is a beautiful celebration of diversity and ecumenism and will inspire hope in us all."

—DAISY KHAN
Executive Director, American Society for Muslim Advancement

"*In Our Own Way* is an inspiring and beautifully diverse book of prayers that Scouts will treasure. Prayer is communion with God and sustains us throughout our whole life. May God bless Dr. Edmonds for his great idea, time, and diligent efforts to bring this wonderful book to fruition!"

—REGINA RAFRAF
Spiritual Assembly of the Bahá'ís of Dallas, Texas

"*In Our Own Way* is a unique compilation of prayers from different religions of the world. This is a first for its direct relevance to Scouting and Scouts. A Scout earning his or her religious recognition will find it particularly valuable. With this book, Dr. Edmonds shows all Scouts that there is a common thread of prayer that exists among different religions, and yet each of them can maintain its own individual character."

—DR. BHUPENDRA HAJRATWALA
President, North American Hindu Association

In Our Own Way

OTHER SCOUT-THEMED BOOKS

by Red Honor Press

Title in Press

We Are Americans, We Are Scouts

Forthcoming Youth and Adult Titles

On My Honor, I Will
THE Blueprint for Integrity-Driven® Leadership

Now I Know That!
101 Fun & Fascinating Things to Explore, Learn, and Share

In Our Own Way

LIVING A SCOUTING LIFE THROUGH FAITH

A HANDBOOK OF PRAYER AND DEVOTION

Edited by ROBERT LEE EDMONDS

RED HONOR™
PRESS

Dallas, Texas

Published by Red Honor Press
An imprint of PenlandScott Publishers.

RED HONOR, RED HONOR PRESS, and colophon are
trademarks of Red Honor Ventures, Ltd.

First Edition 2008
10   9   8   7   6   5   4   3   2

Red Honor Press publications are available at special discounted rates for
volume and bulk purchases, corporate and institutional premiums, promotions,
fund-raising, and educational uses. For further information, contact:

Red Honor Press
P.O. Box 166677
Irving, Texas 75016

specialsales@redhonor.com

Design and layout by *the*BookDesigners.
Front cover illustration by Dorit Rabinovitch.

Printed and bound in the United States of America.

Library of Congress Control Number: 2007939539

ISBN-10: 0-9789-8362-9
ISBN-13: 978-0-9789-8362-8

Get informed & inspired at
www.redhonorpress.com

www.penlandscott.com

Great Spirit, You have been always,
and before You no one has been.
There is no other one to pray to but You. . . .
You where the sun shines continually,
You in the depths of the Heavens,
an eagle of power, behold!

Excerpt from a prayer by Black Elk,
an Oglala Lakota (Sioux) Holy Man (1863–1950)

CONTENTS

PREFACE

SCOUTING IS DEEPLY INVESTED IN SPIRITUALITY. The importance of reverent faith in our Creator has always been part of the Boy Scout philosophy. Lord Robert S.S. Baden-Powell once wrote that religion is life itself at its best and every Scout should treat it as a manner of everyday life.[i] Baden-Powell believed that duty to one's faith means recognizing who and what God is, making the best of the life God has provided, and doing what God wants for us and others.[ii] These devout obligations remain today essential to the purpose of the Scouting movement in building the foundation for a Scout's spiritual, moral, and social growth.

Baden-Powell's core vision of faithful service to God as fundamental to developing honorable qualities in youth shaped the framework of this book. *In Our Own Way* features an anthology of prayers selected and composed by national religious leaders representing many faith traditions and denominations participating in the religious emblems program of the Boy Scouts of America. This special compilation is organized within three categories that embody the traditional ideals of Scouting: reverence toward God, building good character, and being prepared to always do your best for yourself and others. In such a way every faith is able to express these principal virtues in the beauty of their own distinctive, divine words.

In Our Own Way celebrates the roots of our Scouting heritage. It is a handbook for all those sharing the spirit of fellowship with Scouts of every creed, custom, and tradition who, for over a century, have known the value of reverence, devotion, and duty in living a worthy, purposeful life.

Robert Lee "Doc" Edmonds
Colleyville, Texas
18 November 2007

INTRODUCTION

ONE EARLY APRIL SUNDAY IN 2006, I had the
privilege of presenting the keynote address for
an Eagle Court of Honor hosted by Troop 758 of
Euless, Texas.

When any Scout receives his Eagle award,
it's a memorable event for all involved. But this
celebration was not just the recognition of one
Boy Scout's achievements—five exceptional Ismaili
Muslim young men were together receiving their
Eagle rank.

The ceremony opened with each Scout reading
a thoughfully chosen prayer in Arabic, followed by
an English translation as a courteous and respectful
gesture to those unacquainted with the language
of Islam. Listening closely, I was moved by the
parallels between these prayerful words, the tenets
of my own beliefs, and the high ideals of Scouting.
In this wonderful expression of ecumenism was
the universal message that God helps us make the
best of our abilities to enrich ourselves and add
to the well-being of others. Here I was witnessing
America's finest youth demonstrating how a diverse
community in harmony share the blessings of our
Creator. This is the brotherhood of Scouting,

a reminder that Scouts of every faith tradition around the world are united in the promise of an honorable life led by duty and devotion to God.

When pledging ourselves to the Scout Oath, Law, motto, and slogan we are agreeing to live a good, steadfast life; this is a condition of our commitment to Scouting. These covenants comprise a blueprint for guiding our actions and strengthening our physical, mental, and spiritual character. Following these codes of good conduct helps us make the right choices to become better individuals, responsible citizens, and able leaders.

By the mid-twentieth century, duty to God was acknowledged worldwide as a Scout's first obligation. From the early formative years, dedication to faith has been Scouting's cornerstone principle to doing one's best. As Scouts we promise to honor God with respectful service, and for the mercy and goodness that is bestowed upon us. And through prayer we follow the traditions of our beliefs to speak to God in affirmation, praise, and gratitude for these divine gifts.

Prayer is a way of expressing our faith. It is a starting point from which we develop our one-to-one relationship with God. Nearly ninety percent of Americans engage in prayer at least once per week; almost sixty percent pray every day or even

several times a day.[i] We use prayer to acknowledge
God's grace and will. We pray for wisdom and
insight when we are in tough situations. We ask for
God's help to set our moral compass and give us the
ability to help others.

Prayer is universal. It is a part of almost every
religion in the world. But it is more than mere
words. Anyone can recite a prayer from this book.
A good prayer—the right prayer—is one felt from
the heart and mind, one that is honest and sincere.
Prayer can be private or shared with others. We
are touched by prayer simply by the act of praying
itself. And with meaningful prayer, a faithful life
can be "caught" and not "taught."[ii]

Our country is a rich tapestry of many
religious traditions. In our schools, communities,
and workplaces, we often interact with people of
different beliefs. With advances in technology and
travel, we are in closer contact with other cultures
more than ever. Significant world events have
affected us all and provided the opportunity, and
the responsibility, to understand customs and creeds
unlike our own.

The Scouting movement favors no one religion
over another. The founders knew that each faith
blesses those who do their best. They wanted Scouts
to share common values and look for ways to work

and live together with others. Today more than thirty-five diverse groups and denominations are represented in the Boy Scouts of America's program for religious awards. Those who work toward these special recognitions learn and appreciate the importance of spiritual service and God's role in their Scouting and daily life.

The reverent actions of Troop 758's five new Eagle Scouts were both an outstanding expression of character, leadership, and citizenship, and the inspiration for this book. These exemplary young men laudably demonstrated how the values of Scouting are discovered and shared in words of faith and devotion among all religious traditions.

In Our Own Way encourages every Scout to grow a personal connection with God and know the benefits and blessings of praying together and for each other. It offers a new approach to living the Scout Oath and Law and gives us an appreciation of the power of prayer on our boundless journey along the Scouting trail.

HOW TO USE THIS BOOK

In Our Own Way IS A HANDBOOK FOR SCOUTS and leaders wanting to explore and discover a Scouting way of life enriched by the presence of our Creator. It is about the ideals of Boy Scouting and about strengthening these morals through our faith and duty to God. It is about knowing how people of different religions seek a virtue-driven life. This exclusive collection of prayers and devotions are meant to show all Scouts how to express their beliefs in a fresh and useful way. It helps reinforce tolerance for the beliefs of others, and foster understanding and cooperation between faith communities.

In Our Own Way is designed to be portable and easily carried in pocket or pack to start each day with a faith-filled prayer. It helps in searching for the right spiritual words when Scouts need a prayerful conversation with God to be at their personal best. Scouts also learn and respect the uniqueness that is God with friends who follow and practice other religious customs.

This book is an inspirational and educational tool for leaders organizing and managing multifaith or similar faith gatherings. It is ideally suited for meetings, camps, outings, ceremonies, Courts of Honor, and leadership training programs. *In Our Own Way* is an important resource in any group setting where people of all faiths come together to celebrate the spirit of Scouting.

In Our Own Way is valuable to parents and mentors for encouraging children to be faithful in their religious duties and discover the merits of prayer. It teaches children how to appreciate differences and build new friendships with peers who worship in other ways.

Scouts of all ages will treasure *In Our Own Way* as a spiritual guide to living the timeless values of Scouting that have shaped millions to live happily, faithfully, and honorably for over 100 years.

"No [person] is much good unless he believes in God and obeys His laws. So every Scout should have a religion."[1]

—*Lord Robert S.S. Baden-Powell, 1908*

CHAPTER ONE

A SCOUT IS REVERENT

Lord Robert Baden-Powell, founder of the international Scouting movement, believed that reverence toward God is respect in its genuine form. He wanted every Scout to be grateful to God and the good things the Creator set aside for our enjoyment. Baden-Powell encouraged Scouts to love and serve God as a way to achieve an honorable and fulfilled life.

In 1911, led by the resolve of James E. West, the first Chief Scout Executive of the Boy Scouts of America, a twelfth point was added to the Scout Law. It is a promise to live and work in harmony with God according to the traditions of our personal and religious beliefs. It also asks us to value the creeds and customs of others, no matter how different they are from our own.

The prayers in this chapter show that we share a common admiration and devotion to God's purity and grace, and a commitment to our faith in everyday life.

African Methodist Episcopal

Lord Almighty, You alone are pure, holy, faithful, and eternal. You inspire us to be more like You in our character and daily attitude striving for holiness and perfection. You have blessed us with fervent faith that inspires humble worship and thankful praise. May we forever be true to the divine call and will for our lives in word and deed. Amen.[2]

Armenian Apostolic

Your mercy is my hope, Lord.

You who are the glorious first light of our eyes and hearts.

You from whom all good deeds and all life come, Turn with compassion toward me and bring my soul joyfully back to You.

For without You, I cannot be transformed anew. Be my guide, Lord, show me the way, Marking the footsteps on the path that leads to You. Amen.[3]

Bahá'í

O God! Refresh and gladden my spirit. Purify my
heart. Illumine my powers. I lay all my affairs in
Thy hand. Thou art my Guide and my Refuge. I
will no longer be sorrowful and grieved; I will be
a happy and joyful being. O God! I will no longer
be full of anxiety, nor will I let trouble harass me.
I will not dwell on the unpleasant things of life.
O God! Thou art more friend to me than I am to
myself. I dedicate myself to Thee, O Lord.[4]

Baptist

Most Gracious God,
Today I stand in Your presence amazed at all of that
You have created.

Give me the strength to see You as I reflect upon my
life and the community.

Stretch me to rely on You in those moments when I
am strong and when I am weak.

Challenge me to never find contentment in a world
that needs helping hands and humble hearts,

yet inspire me to be the change and a light where all who are lost can find acceptance because through me they saw You. Use me to honor You. Amen.[5]

Buddhist

Faith is the source of the Way, and the mother of merit and virtue.

It grows and matures all wholesome Dharmas.

It cuts through the net of doubts and leaves the flow of love.

It opens up the highest road to Nirvana.

Faith has no turbidity, no stain. It purifies the mind.

It eradicates arrogance, it is the basis of respect.

Faith is the primary asset of the Dharma treasure.

It purifies the hands; one can then begin to practice.

With faith, one can give and the mind will not be stingy.

In faith, one can happily enter the Buddha Dharma.

With faith, one's wisdom and merit and virtue all increase.

With faith, one can certainly arrive at the ground of the Thus Come One.

Faith causes all roots to grow pure and clean and sharp.

Faith's power is solid; nothing can destroy it.

Faith eradicates the roots of afflictions forever.

With faith, one can concentrate on the Buddha's merit and virtue.

With faith, one is not attached to any state of being.

Far apart from difficulties, the faithful one becomes untroubled.

Faith can leap over the many roads of demons to reveal the high road to liberation.

Faith is the indestructible seed of merit and virtue.

Faith can grow a Bodhi-tree.

Faith can increase the most victorious wisdom.

Faith can reveal all Buddhas.

Therefore, when speaking of reliable practices in their proper order, the bliss of faith is the victor.

It is the finest of rarities.[6]

Catholic

Lord Jesus, let me know myself; and let me know You, and desire nothing else but You.

Let me love myself only if I love You, and do all things for Your sake.

Let me humble myself and exalt You.

Let me die to myself and live in You, and accept whatever happens as coming from You.

Let me forsake myself and walk after You, and ever desire to follow You.

Let me flee from myself and turn to You, so that I might be saved by You.

Let me fear for myself, let me fear You, and be counted among those whom You have chosen.

Let me distrust myself and trust in You, and ever obey for the love of You.

Let me cling to nothing but You, and ever be poor because of You.

Look upon me that I may love You, call me, that I may see You, and forever possess You, for all eternity.[7]

Christian Church (Disciples of Christ)

O Lord, I am amazed at how wonderfully made I am.

I am amazed not only with me, but the entire universe; the birds of the air, the fish of the sea; the animals that roam the grassland and forest.

As I travel, I am amazed by the seashore, the grassland and forest, and the mountains.

My faith is renewed as I look about me, and I want to fall on my knees or raise my hands or shout at the top of my lungs my thanksgivings for all of these wonderful gifts You have given me.

May I live my life in that thankful mode each and every day.

May I always give thanks to You and take nothing for granted.

This we pray in Christ's name, Your greatest gift to us. Amen.[8]

Church of Christ, Scientist
(Christian Science)

Here let me give what I understand to be the spiritual sense of the Lord's Prayer:[9]

Our Father which art in heaven,
  Our Father-Mother God, all harmonious,

Hallowed be Thy name.
  Adorable One.

Thy kingdom come.
  Thy kingdom is come; Thou art ever-present.

Thy will be done in earth, as it is in heaven.
  Enable us to know, as in heaven, so on earth, God is omnipotent, supreme.

Give us this day our daily bread;
  Give us grace for today; feed the famished affections;

And forgive us our debts, as we forgive our debtors.
  And Love is reflected in love;

And lead us not into temptation, but deliver us from evil;
  And God leadeth us not into temptation, but delivereth us from sin, disease, and death.

For Thine is the kingdom, and the power, and the glory, forever.

For God is infinite, all-power, all Life, Truth, Love, over all, and All.

The Daily Prayer

"Thy kingdom come"; let the reign of divine Truth, Life, and Love be established in me, and rule out of me all sin; and may Thy Word enrich the affections of all mankind, and govern them! [10]

Two of the foundational points of prayer in Mary Baker Eddy's book Science and Health with Key to the Scriptures *is that prayer is an affirmation of God's goodness already operating in our lives—of the kingdom of heaven "at hand"—and that God knows our needs before we ask. Prayer in Christian Science recognizes God as all-powerful, as Love itself, as all substance, Spirit, and man (including all men, women, and children) as the "image and likeness" of this God, good, which is revealed by the Christ. Christian Scientists rely on these universal truths as the basis for their healthcare, happiness, and harmony. For Christian Scientists, prayer is often specific to the condition being treated (just as a medical treatment would be), though prayer in more general terms for world issues or events are just as important.*

Church of Jesus Christ
of Latter-day Saints (Mormon)

O, remember, my son, and learn wisdom in
thy youth; yea, learn in thy youth to keep the
commandments of God.

Yea, and cry unto God for all thy support; yea, let all
thy doings be unto the Lord, and whithersoever thou
goest, let it be in the Lord; yea, let all thy thoughts
be directed unto the Lord; yea, let the affections of
thy heart be placed upon the Lord forever.

Counsel with the Lord in all thy doings, and he will
direct thee for good; yea, when thou liest down at
night lie down unto the Lord, that he may watch
over you in your sleep; and when thou risest in the
morning let thy heart be full of thanks unto God;
and if ye do these things, ye shall be lifted up at
the last day.[11]

*The Church of Jesus Christ of Latter-day Saints has
only three memorized prayers; two at the Sacrament
and the baptismal prayer. The Mormon Church
encourages its members to pray from the heart as
a sincere effort to speak with God.*

*A personal Mormon prayer generally includes the
following expressions of reverence:*

Our Heavenly Father
We thank Thee
We ask Thee
In the name of Jesus Christ. Amen.

Churches of Christ

Our mighty Father in Heaven, hear this prayer we offer as we humbly approach Your throne knowing we cannot go anywhere without You.

From rocky mountains to dusty plains;
Raging rivers to deep blue oceans;
Rolling green hills to majestic forests;
Magnificent canyons to musty swamps.

You breathe life into every living thing we see;
From hummingbirds to grizzly bears;
Tender mushrooms to towering redwoods;
From misty sunrise to red splashed sunset;
We find Your handprint everywhere we look.

Even the cool evening breeze whispers Your power and love into our ears.

Father, help us to see You everywhere we look;
Confirm in us a respect for Your creation that reflects our awe of You.

May we accept the charge of service to creation and
each other with sincere and humble hearts.
In the name of Jesus we pray. Amen.[12]

Community Churches

Good God, grant us inspiration to creatively do
our part in making this a better world for all its
inhabitants, grace to realize that our efforts are
inadequate without Your support, and acceptance
of the results of our actions, whether we succeed or
fail, knowing we have given our all and done our
best. Amen.[13]

Community of Christ

O God of faith, we acknowledge Your presence and
being in our lives and community. Truly, it is the
experience of Your presence that has allowed us to
become aware of the wonders of Your creation and
the potential for great good with which You have
endowed us all.

Bless us together as we pledge the dedication of our
lives to Your teachings, we pray. Amen.[14]

Eastern Orthodox

Heavenly King, Comforter, Spirit of Truth—You are everywhere, fulfilling all things. Treasury of blessings and Giver of life, come and live in us, cleanse us from every impurity, Good One, and save our souls.[15]

Episcopal

Accept, O Lord, our thanks and praise for all that You have done for us.

We thank You for the splendor of the whole creation, for the beauty of this world, for the wonder of life, and for the mystery of love.

We thank You for the blessing of family and friends, and for the loving care that surrounds us on every side.

We thank You for setting us at tasks that demand our best efforts, and for leading us to accomplishments which satisfy and delight us.

We thank You for those disappointments and failures that lead us to acknowledge our dependence on You.

Above all, we thank You for Your Son, Jesus Christ; for the truth of His Word and the example of His life; for His steadfast obedience, by which He overcame temptation; for His dying, through which He overcame death; and for His rising to life again, in which we are raised to the life of Your kingdom.

Grant us the gift of Your Spirit, that we may know Christ and make Him known; and through Him, at all times and in all places, may give thanks to You in all things. Amen.[16]

General Church of the New Jerusalem (The New Church)

O Lord, we rejoice that Your Divine mercy is pure mercy toward the whole human race to save it; that it is unceasing toward every person and never withdrawn from anyone. We are grateful that You save and bring into Your Heavenly Kingdom everyone who can be saved. May Your Kingdom come![17]

Hindu

O! Lord! You are my father as well as my mother.
You are my brother as well as my friend.
O! Lord! You are my knowledge as well as my
wealth. You are everything to me, O! Lord![18]

Islamic

And unto God belongs all that is in the heavens and
all that is on earth. And indeed, we have enjoined
upon those who were granted revelation before
your time, as well as upon yourselves, to remain
conscious of God. And if you deny Him—behold:
unto God belongs all that is in the heavens and all
that is on earth, and God is indeed self-sufficient,
ever to be praised.[19]

Jewish

Master of all worlds! Not upon our merit do we
rely in our supplication, but upon Your limitless
love. What are we? What is our life? What is
our piety? What is our righteousness? What is
our attainment, our power, our might: what can

we say, Lord our God and God of our ancestors?
Compared to You, all the mighty are nothing, the
famous are nonexistent, the wise lack wisdom,
the clever lack reason, for most of their actions
are meaningless, the days of their lives emptiness.
Human preeminence over beasts is an illusion when
all is seen as futility.

But we are Your people, partners to Your covenant,
descendants of Your beloved Abraham to whom You
made a pledge on Mount Moriah. We are the heirs
of Isaac, his son bound upon the altar. We
are Your firstborn people, the congregation of
Isaac's son Jacob whom You named Israel and
Jeshurun because of Your love for him and Your
delight in him.

Therefore, it is our duty to thank You and praise
You, to glorify and sanctify Your name. How
good is our portion, how pleasant our lot, how
beautiful our heritage. How blessed are we that
twice each day, morning and evening, we are
privileged to declare:

Hear, O Israel: the Lord our God, the Lord is one.

Praised be His glorious sovereignty throughout
all time.[20]

Lutheran

Dear Almighty and loving God:
You call us into the world through water and the
Spirit that we might love and serve You and treat
our neighbors as we would be treated.

Please assist us in our efforts to respect Your
children, show reverence in our communities,
and work diligently toward a world of justice
and peace. Guide our hearts and minds, our
thoughts and actions toward courage in our
public commitments and reverence in our silent
convictions. Be with us in weakness and strength,
challenge and success, heartache and homecoming.

In all things draw us through Your love to a world
yearning for reverence for all creation and a desire
for peace in the fellowship of Your children. In the
name of the One who calls to us. Amen.[21]

Meher Baba

O my soul of soul!
I believe in Thee, because thou art truth itself;

I worship Thee, O highest of the high because Thou
art the only one worthy of adoration;
I love Thee above all things and beings because
Thou art love divine itself;
I beseech Thee because Thou art mercy itself;
I offer Thee all my thoughts, words, and actions, my
sufferings and my joys because Thou art the only
Beloved.[22]

Methodist

O God, my hope and in whom is all happiness:

Grant this persistent request. Show to me, and all
those around, Your goodness and Your mercy.

When I stand before the storms and hear the wind
and feel the earth tremble, may I have eyes of faith
to see Your grace. Cover me with Your mighty hand
and hide me with Your coat of comfort.

Declare Your name, God of love, to my listening
ears and light a fire in my heart with Your presence.
With confidence in Jesus' name, receive me in
that place beside Your throne, where all who find
acceptance stand. Amen.[23]

Moravian

Almighty, eternal God, I stand atop a mountain
where I can see for miles, or I crawl into a cave so
dark that I cannot see my hand before my eyes,
but I know You are here with me. You created all
these things, and in Your perfect love gave them
to us all to use and pass down for others to see as
Your handiwork. But it is in my own experience
of Your gifts that I am called to faith and to act in
such a way to honor You as Creator of all things
and all life from the most brilliant heights to the
darkest of depths. You are God and I am a creature
who stands in awe. May all I say and do reflect my
devotion and respect for You, Your creation, and
Your gifts to all people.[24]

Native American

O Great Spirit of the Heavens,
In the day's infinite blue and amid the countless
stars of the night season, remind us that You are
vast, that You are beautiful and majestic beyond
all of our knowing or telling, but also that You are
no further from us than the tilting upward of our
heads and the raising of our eyes.[25]

Pentecostal

Lord God Almighty,
All of creation reflects Your divine beauty and
glory. Our lives are deeply touched by Your caring
and gracious presence and influence. All that we
have and are is in Your hands. The most mundane
daily activity seems sacred in Your presence. You
are an awesome God! We lift You up on high! You
are the Lord of all life, the God of the spirits of all
humankind. The entry of Your Son into our world
tells us You are not far from any of us—not cold
or distant but warm and near. We are so thankful
for the fullness of Your Spirit and power. When
we pray we know our words are heard on high. So
then, ever-present Spirit, help us not to go through
our days failing to see with eyes of faith that God
is everywhere around us, in us, and in others,
often even in those unlike ourselves. Teach us to
walk in Your ways. Heal us and make us whole,
Lord, in body and in soul. Bless and prosper us
according to Your abundance and providence.
Help us use wisely whatever spiritual gifts You
entrust to our stewardship. Give us victory over
evil in all its forms and deliverance from evil
principalities and powers. Thank You, Lord. We

humbly acknowledge and honor You. We do not
offer outward observances only, which can become
empty or hollow, but revere and worship You
from our heart with all our energies. Praise God!
Hallelujah! Amen.[26]

Presbyterian

O God,
Light of the minds that know You,
Life of the souls that love You,
Strength of the thoughts that seek You:
Help us to know You so that we may truly love You,
And so in loving You we may fully serve You,
Whose service is perfect freedom;
Through Jesus Christ our Lord. Amen.[27]

Religious Society of Friends (Quaker)

Dear Lord and Father of mankind,
Forgive our foolish ways!
Reclothe us in our rightful mind,
In purer lives Thy service find,
In deeper reverence, praise.

In simple trust like theirs who heard,
Beside the Syrian sea,
The gracious calling of the Lord,
Let us, like them, without a word,
Rise up and follow Thee.

O Sabbath rest by Galilee!
O calm of hills above,
Where Jesus knelt to share with Thee
The silence of eternity
Interpreted by love!

Drop Thy still dews of quietness,
Till all our strivings cease;
Take from our souls the strain and stress,
And let our ordered lives confess
The beauty of Thy peace.

Breathe through the heats of our desire
Thy coolness and Thy balm;
Let sense be dumb, let flesh retire;
Speak through the earthquake, wind, and fire,
O still, small voice of calm! [28]

The Salvation Army

Heavenly Father,
In reverence and humility I approach the throne of
Your grace in prayer. You are the Creator, Preserver,
and Governor of all things and You alone are worthy
of my worship. From everlasting to everlasting You
are God. You are all-knowing, all-powerful, and
everywhere present.

Lord Jesus, help me to always revere You for You
are my Savior from sin and my never-failing friend.
Holy Spirit, You are my divine counselor, comforter,
and guide. Help me use with great reverence the
spiritual gifts You have given me.

O triune God, grant the desire of my heart that
my life may be an offering of praise to You alone.
Amen.[29]

Unity Churches

The light of God surrounds me;
The love of God enfolds me;
The power of God protects me;
The presence of God watches over me.
Wherever I am, God is![30]

Zoroastrian

I worship You by developing my good mind so that
I may learn the difference between right and wrong.
I worship You by standing for what is right and
good and against what is deceitful and evil.
I worship You by actions of righteousness.
I worship You in every man and woman who seeks
to follow Your way of righteousness.

The Lord's Prayer

Our Father, who art in Heaven,
Hallowed be Thy name;
Thy kingdom come;
Thy will be done on earth as it is in heaven.
Give us this day our daily bread;
and forgive us our trespasses,
as we forgive those who trespass against us;
and lead us not into temptation,
but deliver us from evil.
For Thine is the kingdom, and the power, and the
glory, for ever and ever. Amen.[31]

"The religion of a man is not the creed he professes but his life—what he acts upon, and knows of life, and his duty in it. . . ."[1]

—*Lord Robert S.S. Baden-Powell, 1921*

CHAPTER TWO

BUILDING STRONG CHARACTER

The early visionaries of the Scout movement knew that from small acorns grow mighty oaks. At the heart of Scouting is the promise to strive toward developing positive personal values with a dedicated sense of responsibility. When reciting the Oath and Law we make a commitment to measure up to Scouting's high ideals in our conduct and actions to grow into responsible adults, productive citizens, and capable leaders.

Reverent faith in God sets a true moral compass guiding us to an honorable and meaningful life. We look to our Creator for the wisdom, courage, and power of spirit to overcome any challenge and reach our full potential.

The prayers in this chapter show that a faithful duty to God gives us the inspiration and purpose to be our best at all times.

African Methodist Episcopal

Lord God, You instill in us the desire for an upright spirit and a clean heart that our conduct might be blameless. Our character becomes the source of our physical, mental, and spiritual strength. The strength that comes from You fortifies us with courage to face life's challenges. May our character and conduct forever please You. Amen.[2]

Armenian Apostolic

We thank You, Lord our God, whose radiant light has brought joy to all creatures
and illumination to all who believe in You.

Strengthen us, Lord, to keep Your commandments today and at all times, so that we always seek to do Your will.

May our own efforts be joined with all the saintly men and women who have lived and died in great faith and good works. Amen.[3]

Bahá'í

O Lord, my God! Assist Thy loved ones to be firm in Thy Faith, to walk in Thy ways, to be steadfast in Thy Cause. Give them Thy grace to withstand the onslaught of self and passion, to follow the light of divine guidance. Thou art the Powerful, the Gracious, the Self-Subsisting, the Bestower, the Compassionate, the Almighty, the All-Bountiful.[4]

Baptist

Loving God who created and ordered this world in utter goodness,

I cast hopeful eyes to You.

I hope for clarity of vision to see this world through the lens of Your love.

I hope for wisdom to know how to take a stand on behalf of those who fall victim to a world damaged by human selfishness and ambition.

I hope for courage to stand against those who would place pride, greed, and partisanship above community, service, and love.

I pray that my hopes would be fulfilled in You. Amen.[5]

Buddhist

I should be a sanctuary for all living beings and cause them to avoid all suffering;

I should be a protector for all living beings and liberate them from all afflictions;

I should be a refuge for all living beings so that all escape fear;

I should be a path for all living beings so that they can reach wisdom;

I should be a peacemaker for all living beings so that all can attain the place of ultimate, secure tranquility;

I should be a light for all living beings and cause them to attain the radiance of wisdom which eradicates the gloom of stupidity;

I should be a torch for all living beings which breaks through the darkness of ignorance;

I should be a lamp for all living beings and cause them to dwell in the place of utmost purity;

I should be a guiding teacher for all living beings and cause them to enter the true, real teachings;

I should be a great guiding teacher for all living beings and give them unobstructed great wisdom.[6]

Catholic

Take, O Lord, and receive all my liberty, my memory, my understanding, and my entire will: all that I have and possess.

You have given them to me, O Lord, now I give them back to You.

All things are Yours: do with them according to Your will.

Give me Your love and Your grace for this is enough for me.[7]

Christian Church (Disciples of Christ)

O Holy God,

I come before You this day knowing that You are holy, knowing that You are perfect in every way.

I come before You seeking to be just like You.

When I was young, I wanted to be just like my father. I wanted to be able to please my parents.

It was easy to do that, when I was younger.

Now, I want to please my friends, who sometimes can lead me astray. It is easy to follow the crowd.

It is easy to fulfill a dare, which I know is wrong, just to be popular.

So I come before You today and ask that You would guide me and help me to make the right decisions for my life.

May I be an example of good, rather than an instrument of evil.

May I do that which would make my parents proud, rather than embarrass them.

May I always do what is right, no matter what pressures are surrounding me.

May I be like Jesus, and even lay down my life for what I believe is right and fair to all. Amen.[8]

Church of Christ, Scientist (Christian Science)

(See Church of Christ, Scientist in Chapter One, p. 8, "A Scout Is Reverent")

Church of Jesus Christ of Latter-day Saints (Mormon)

(See Church of Jesus Christ of Latter-day Saints in Chapter One, p. 10, "A Scout Is Reverent")

Churches of Christ

Dearest Father, our Savior and Guide:
We praise Your name above every name, over all
the earth, over all the sky, over all creation. We
are Your unique creation, and we bow to serve and
worship You.

As we begin our day, Lord; we pray to You for
guidance.
At the close of our daily toils, we thank You
for protecting us from the world which tries to
swallow us.
As we lay down each night, knowing that You
provide rest for those who love You,
we thank You for providing the skill and knowledge
needed to face the challenges of each day.

We ask You:
> For wisdom, in our preparations to serve You,
> our families, and our brother Scouts;
> For endurance and strength to overcome the evil
> one and the challenges he throws before us.
> For patience to humbly accept Your will, even
> as we attempt to swallow our pride over our
> earthly successes,
> To lead us through the trails of life; and as we
> touch the lives of those we pass,
> may we be prepared to help, to comfort, to

defend if necessary, all those who are in need.
Always giving Glory and Honor to You, O Lord.

As we look to Jesus as our Savior and Guide,
May we ever be His servant by serving others.
May all our deeds reflect the love of Christ, and
May our actions bring a blessing to those around us.

Yes, Lord, today as Scouts, we prepare for our role
as adults in an unloving and uncertain world.
May we gain strength from Your Holy Word as
we speak with You in prayer over every decision
we make. Forgive us when we fall short, lift us up
when we are discouraged and allow us to do the
same for those around us.

In Jesus' Most Holy Name we pray, Amen.[9]

Community Churches

Good God, because life is often confusing and
difficult, we seek the strength and courage
necessary to make it as meaningful and complete
as possible not just for ourselves but also for all
those we touch with our presence. Grant us, then,
a portion of Your power as we seek to serve You by
serving others and enable us to act with honor in
all we do. Amen.[10]

Community of Christ

We search for heaven's wisdom and courage;
    Our path is uncertain;
    Give us light;
    Show us the way;
    Cast Your light
    Upon the trail of our earthly vow.
    We seek answers of the where, when, and how;
    In Spirit's light, help us find Your way.

We vision the path of the One You have chosen;
    In garden's quiet,
    He goes to pray.
    He kneels to talk,
    To listen,
    To find Your way.

Light fills the void of night's darkness.
    The soul weeps but the course He must stay.
    "Not my will but Thy will be done" is clearly
    heard.
    Love's hand heals as He is led away.

    Look! A blush of light on yonder horizon;
    In another garden,
    An empty tomb welcomes the new day.
    The world warms,

Blooms at the touch of sun's rays.
Life is The Light and Light reveals The Way.

As Scouts of valor, Lord,
Help us honor Your Light;
Fill us with courage as we have need to be.

In fear or doubt or uncertainty
In dark of night,
When we would want to take flight,
Help us hold high the candle
That we might see
The path of righteousness
That we walk with Thee.
Cast Your light,
Warm our hearts,
Set us free.

Grace our lives with wonder and insight,
Our lives a beacon of courage and wisdom be;
Even as He who went to a Garden called
Gethsemane.
In the spirit and courage of such a One, we
pray. Amen.[11]

Eastern Orthodox

Lord, I don't know what to ask from You. Only You know what I really need. You love me more than I know how to love. Help me to see the things I really need, even though they may be hidden from me. I don't know whether to ask You for comfort in my troubles or for a cross to bear. I can only wait for You to decide. My heart is open to You. Visit me and help me for the sake of Your great mercy. You may hit me with problems or heal me; throw me down or raise me up. Your ways cannot be understood, and so I worship Your Holy Will in silence. I offer up myself as a sacrifice to You while putting all my trust in You. I want nothing else but to do Your will. Teach me what I should pray for and pray Yourself in me. Amen.[12]

Episcopal

Almighty and eternal God,
So draw our hearts to You,
So guide our minds,
So fill our imaginations,
So control our wills that we may be wholly Yours,
utterly dedicated to You,
And then use us, we pray, as You will,
And always in Your glory and the welfare of Your
people;
Through our Lord and Savior Jesus Christ. Amen.[13]

General Church of the New Jerusalem (The New Church)

O Lord, help me resolve to live the life that leads
to heaven, for the passing delight and bliss of a life
in time are but a fleeting shadow when compared
with the never-ending delight and bliss of a life in
eternity.[14]

Hindu

O Lord! You are magnificent, inspiring, eternal, the greatest purifier, and all pervading.

O Lord! Nothing higher than You exists. This entire universe is strung on You like pearls on a thread.

O Lord! Bestow Your grace on me, dwell in my heart, and dispel the darkness of ignorance by the light of knowledge and wisdom.[15]

Islamic

Our Lord! I seek divine guidance so that I may remain steadfast in what is just.

I seek divine guidance in order to be firm in righteousness.

I seek from You a tongue that speaks the truth and a heart which is pure and clean.

I seek divine guidance in the manner that I express my gratitude for Your favor and worship with devotion.[16]

Jewish

Fulfill the worthy wishes of my heart, O Lord;
grant me Your servant and my entire family the
privilege of doing Your will wholeheartedly. Help us
to overcome the impulse to evil. Let Your Torah be
our portion. Grant us the privilege of sensing Your
Presence. Touch our lives with the spirit of wisdom
and insight, of resolution and strength, the spirit
of knowing and revering You. May it be Your will,
Lord our God and God of our ancestors, that we
have the privilege of doing deeds which are good
in Your sight, walking in paths of honesty. Make
our lives holy through Your commandments that we
may be worthy of a long and happy life, as well as
life eternal. Guard us from the evil deeds and the
evil times which threaten the world. May those who
trust in the Lord be embraced by loving kindness.
Amen.

May the words of my mouth and the meditations
of my heart be acceptable to You, O Lord, my Rock
and my Redeemer. I offer my prayer to You, O
Lord, at this time of grace. In Your abundant mercy
answer me with Your saving truth.[17]

Lutheran

You are a God who places great potential in Your smallest creation. From the acorn that becomes the seasoned and mighty oak tree, we too are being drawn up into our own maturity. Let us be renewed in seasons of prosperity and steadfast in seasons of drought. Let us learn from past pain how to experience joy in the present. Let us understand how failed relationships yesterday help us to endure in hope for friendships today and tomorrow. Let us grow tall and in singular purpose—to stand with integrity, determination, and character in the created order of things. Allow us to be flexible in the wind but rooted in the earth, O God of acorns, and the mighty oak. Amen.[18]

Meher Baba

Upon the altar of humility we must offer our prayers to God. Humility is spiritually of greater worth than devotion. It is easier to be devout than to be humble, but devotion in many instances proves to be a stepping-stone to humility.[19]

Methodist

One thing I desire with all my being, loving God,
and will I seek and pursue: grant me to know what
Your own Spirit would inspire me, Your servant,
to do. Do not leave me alone with grief, gracious
God, or abandon me even if my friends and family
do. When I am weary and troubled by memories of
the past, bring to my mind all of the goodness and
benefits that are mine in You. Grant me courage,
grant me patience, and grant me redemption
through Your Son, Jesus Christ. Amen.[20]

Moravian

Lord God, in weakness I come to You knowing that
Your love and Your Spirit will supplant my own
inadequacies. I confess: I am weak, You are strong; I
don't always know how to forgive, Your forgiveness
knows no limits; and I become filled with fears, but
Your presence gives me peace. I have come to trust
that the red end of my compass needle points to the
north, may I always trust that Your love will point
me in the right direction. When I diverge from the
course whether by spectacular view or curiosity,

lead me back into the right path. When my
resolve softens, refresh my determination to follow
obediently as Your servant regardless of the obstacle
or temptation.[21]

Native American

Oh, Great Spirit, whose voice I hear in the winds,
and whose breath gives life to all the world, hear me!

I come to You as one of Your many children;
I am weak and small.
I need Your wisdom and Your strength.

Let me walk in beauty,
and make my eyes ever behold the red and purple
sunsets.

Make my hands respect
the things You have made,
and make my ears sharp so I may hear Your voice.

Make me wise so I may understand the things You
have taught my people. Let me learn the lessons You
have hidden in every leaf and rock.

I ask for wisdom and strength
not to be greater than my brothers and sisters,
but to fight my greatest enemy—myself.

Make me always ready
to come before You with clean hands and a straight eye,

So as life fades away, as a fading sunset,
my spirit may come to You without shame.[22]

Pentecostal

Precious Holy Spirit, please indwell and infill us
so that the light of God's glory and goodness may
shine in our thoughts, words, and deeds. Grant
us grace to both experience and honor Your holy
presence ourselves and to inspire others by our
example to do so as well. Heavenly Father, we need
Your strength to be what You would have us be
and do what You would have us do. Guide and
lead us in reaching for the destiny for which we
are divinely designed. Help us to always try to do
the right thing—even when it may not be easy or
make us popular. We wish to honor You not only
with words but with deeds. We want not only
to be blessed but also to be a blessing to others.
We especially ask for Your Spirit's anointing to
enable us to show love to those unlike ourselves.
Empower us by Your Spirit to be good neighbors
to those who speak a different language or share
different customs, and to those of a different race

or religion. Yet we do not attempt to stand before the Almighty as our own achievement. We are sorry for our shortcomings and sins. We honestly ask for forgiveness if we fail. And we are assured of acceptance in Your compassion, love, and mercy for Christ's sake. We joyfully choose to place our faith and trust in You. You are so amazing! Above all, we glorify You according to Your infinite goodness and greatness. In Jesus' name we pray. Amen.[23]

Presbyterian

Gracious Lord, we are stumbling disciples, but we are trying. There is a strong pull to follow the crowd, go with the flow; we are too easily drawn away from You and Your life-giving way. By Your Spirit, give us eyes to see the path that You have set before us—we don't want to be blind to the abundant life You have in store for us. Grant us the humble courage to follow Christ—we don't want to be arrogant, thinking we know a better way. And as we travel, bless us with light for our journey, so that we can see You are ever before us.

In the name of Jesus, Light of the world, we pray. Amen.[24]

Religious Society of Friends (Quaker)

There is a spirit which I feel that delights to do no evil, nor to revenge any wrong, but delights to endure all things, in hope to enjoy its own in the end. Its hope is to outlive all wrath and contention and to weary out all exaltation and cruelty or whatever is of a nature contrary to itself. It sees to the end of all temptations. As it bears no evil in itself, so it conceives none in thoughts to any other. If it be betrayed, it bears it, for its ground and spring are the mercies and forgiveness of God.[25]

The Salvation Army

Gracious God, hear my prayer today. I ask that You mold my character after the likeness of Your Son, Jesus Christ.

May the values of Your kingdom, Lord Jesus, be evident in the way I live my life. By Your Spirit's work in me, may I be more like You every day. I want to be merciful and compassionate, humble and meek, pure in heart, hungry and thirsty for Your righteousness, sensitive to those who are hurting, and a peacemaker in a world so often in strife. Amen.[26]

Unity Churches

God is my help in every need;
God does my every hunger feed;
God walks beside me, guides my way
Through every moment of the day.

I now am wise, I now am true,
Patient, kind, and loving too.
All things I am, can do, and be,
Through Christ, the Truth that is in me.

God is my health, I can't be sick;
God is my strength, unfailing, quick;
God is my all, I know no fear,
Since God and love and Truth are here.[27]

Zoroastrian

We revere Good Thoughts, Good Words, Good
Deeds done and to be done,
Now and henceforth.
We are, accordingly, the praisers
And invokers of all that is good.[28]

The Serenity Prayer

God grant me the serenity
to accept the things I cannot change;
courage to change the things I can;
and wisdom to know the difference.[29]

"Reverence to God and reverence for one's neighbor and reverence for oneself as a servant of God is the basis of every form of religion."[1]

—*Lord Robert S.S. Baden-Powell, 1919*

CHAPTER THREE

BEING PREPARED

The Boy Scout motto is our call to always be ready to do the best for ourselves, our homes, our communities, and our country. Following this Scouting maxim builds our mind and body with the strength, understanding, and desire to do what is necessary and right at the right time.

Affirming God's role in everyday life inspires us to make sound moral decisions and dutifully deal with any situation. Importantly, our faith oversees every good deed and action with reason and compassion, rewarding us with knowing that we have met our obligations with honor and respect.

The prayers in this chapter reveal that God helps every Scout prepare to follow a path of goodness and be in service to those in need.

African Methodist Episcopal

Almighty God, receive the humble praise of our
hearts. Convict us with a mind and spirit of service
to all creation. Commit us to remember that You
served us while we were needy. Consecrate us with
readiness for the challenges and crises of today that
our lives might fulfill Your purposes. Amen.[2]

Armenian Apostolic

O Lord, Grant me wisdom,
That I may always think, speak, and do
That which is good in Your sight.
Keep me from evil thoughts, words, and deeds.
Have mercy upon all Your creatures and upon me,
A humble sinner. Amen.[3]

Bahá'í

O my God! O my God! Unite the hearts of Thy
servants, and reveal to them Thy great purpose.
May they follow Thy commandments and abide in
Thy law. Help them, O God, in their endeavor, and

grant them strength to serve Thee. O God! Leave
them not to themselves but guide their steps by
the light of Thy knowledge and cheer their hearts
by Thy love. Verily, Thou art their Helper and
their Lord.[4]

Baptist

God, I need Your help.
Can You help prepare me to meet every challenge
that I might face? If my neighbors are hurting, help
me to nurture their pain so that they might find
comfort in the care. Help me apply my education
to the world around me. Help me see life through
Your lens so that I can take all that You have
invested in me and share it with those around me.
God, I need Your help and I believe that You can
help me. God, if You don't mind, in this moment of
prayer, prepare me to hear Your voice and grant me
opportunities to respond.[5]

Buddhist

May all living beings ever be peaceful and happy,
free of sickness and of suffering. May no one
succeed in doing any evil but may everyone quickly
perfect the cultivation of good karma. May the
doors close to the evil destinies and open wide to
the right roads of humanity, the heavens, and of
Nirvana. May I stand in for beings and receive all
the extremely bitter retributions they ought to bring
on to themselves resulting from their evil karma.
May I liberate all these beings and ultimately bring
them to accomplish Unsurpassed Bodhi.[6]

Catholic

Lord, make me an instrument of Your peace;
Where there is hatred, let me sow love;
where there is injury, pardon;
where there is doubt, faith;
where there is despair, hope;
where there is darkness, light;
and where there is sadness, joy.

O Divine Master, grant that I may not so much seek
to be consoled, as to console,
to be understood, as to understand,
to be loved, as to love.

For it is in giving that we receive;
it is in pardoning that we are pardoned;
and it is in dying that we are born to Eternal Life.
Amen.[7]

Christian Church (Disciples of Christ)

O Lord, I know that it takes more than luck to be
prepared. It takes more than being in the right place
at the right time, to know what to do.

So I come before You this day to ask You to help me
to be prepared.

Help me to be brave and to do what is right.

Help me to seek the education that would give me
the tools to help others in need.

Help me to realize that "The servant of all is the
greatest of all!"

So help me to be humble.

Help me not to chase after positions of power but positions of servanthood.

Help me to prepare for the future by being a good student.

Help me to be a good steward.

And fill me with love that will flow freely from me. This we ask for in the name of Christ. Amen.[8]

Church of Christ, Scientist (Christian Science)

(See Church of Christ, Scientist in Chapter One, p. 8 "A Scout Is Reverent")

Church of Jesus Christ of Latter-day Saints (Mormon)

(See Church of Jesus Christ of Latter-day Saints in Chapter One, p. 10, "A Scout Is Reverent")

Churches of Christ

Lord, help me to be prepared,
To put You first, and to ask that You order my life,
So that I may plan and organize for tomorrow,
That I may be able to bless those whom You bring
across my path.

Equip me with the fruit of the Spirit,
the breastplate of Righteousness,
and the sword of Truth.

Direct my heart in mercy and peace,
Grant me joy in service to others,
Stir my mind, to understand Your Word,
Move my hands and feet in service to others.
Oh God of our tomorrows,
Give me grace and peace,
a Spirit of Hope,
and, the gift of encouragement.

Thank You for preparing me for this day.[9]

Community Churches

Good God, make us ready for whatever life throws
our way. Help us turn obstacles into opportunities
and challenges into accomplishments. Let us look
at others and realize they are our brothers and
sisters . . . all part of the same human family.
Guide us along paths of service as we strive to be
productive citizens of Your kingdom. Amen.[10]

Community of Christ

Dear God:

I have learned that the unexpected always comes
with urgency.

In that moment there is no time to prepare.

May I practice skills now so they will come readily
to mind when they are needed.

May my trust in You for ordinary events prepare
me for the times when the extraordinary makes
trust seem difficult. Amen.[11]

Eastern Orthodox

Lord, let me greet the coming day in peace. Help me to rely on Your holy will in everything I meet along the way. Reveal Your will to me throughout the day. Bless my dealings with everyone around me. Teach me to treat everything that comes my way, all day long, with peace in my heart. Give me a firm belief that Your will directs all things. Guide my thoughts and feelings in all my words and deeds. If something unexpected happens, may I not forget that everything comes from You. Teach me to be firm, yet wise, without making anyone feel bitter or embarrassed. Even when I feel tired, give me the strength to bear everything the coming day may bring. Guide my will. Teach me what I should pray for and pray Yourself in me. Amen.[12]

Episcopal

O God, You made us in Your own image and
redeemed us through Jesus Your Son:
Look with compassion on the whole human family;
Take away the arrogance and hatred which infect
our human hearts;
Break down the walls that separate us;
Unite us in bonds of love;
And work through our struggle and confusion to
accomplish Your purposes on earth;
That, in Your good time, all nations and all races,
may serve You in harmony around Your heavenly
throne; through Jesus Christ our Lord. Amen.[13]

General Church of the New Jerusalem (The New Church)

O Lord, be with me continually, life up and turn
Your face to me that You may teach, enlighten, and
lead me, for of myself I can do nothing that is good.[14]

Hindu

Om! May the Lord protect us both by revealing the
true knowledge.
May He declare us safe through the results of true
knowledge.
May we both attain vigor together and let our
studies be invigorating.
May we not quibble at each other.
Om! Let there be Peace on earth, Peace in the
Heavens, and Peace in all the spaces in between.[15]

Islamic

Our Lord! Bestow on us endurance and make our
foothold sure.[16]
Our Lord! Forgive us if we forget or fall into error.[17]
Our Lord! Impose not on us that which we have not
the strength to bear, grant us forgiveness, and have
mercy on us.[18]
Our Lord! Lay open the truth between us and our
people for You are the best of all to lay open the
truth.[19]
Our Lord! Perfect our light for us and forgive us our
sins for verily You have power over all things.[20]

Jewish

May He who blessed our ancestors, Abraham, Isaac, and Jacob, Sarah, Rebecca, Rachel, and Leah, bless this entire holy congregation, together with all holy congregations: them, their sons and daughters, their families, and all that is theirs, along with all those who unite to establish houses of gathering for prayer, and those who enter them to pray, and those who provide light, and wine for sanctification, bread to the wayfarer and charity to the poor, and all who devotedly involve themselves with the needs of this community with deep faith. May the Holy One, praised be God, reward them; may God remove sickness from them, heal them, and forgive their sins. May God bless them by prospering all their worthy endeavors, as well as those of all peoples along with Israel. And let us say: Amen.[21]

Lutheran

Dear God,
Prepare me with the courage to keep my honor
bright, the faithfulness to seek my purpose and
life, and the steadfastness to ready my heart and
mind to Your plan. Steady my doubt where I can
seek honor and live a dutiful life. Let my daily
joy reflect my desire to assist others in Your sight.
May virtue, leadership, and discipline be my
guide. May patience, humility, and mercy
be at my side. Help me serve country and family,
friends and community in hospitality, grace, and
clear-headedness. May it be my custom to go
outdoors each day among the trees and grass and
all living things. May I alone in that place enter
into prayer. May I seek Your living will
in the world, as an instrument of Your peace.
Oh Gracious God, Amen.[22]

Meher Baba

May Thy will be done, O Perfect one,
my will not prevail.
It is of no avail where union with Thee is concerned.
I will toil and I will strive while I am alive
to love and obey all night and all day
till union with Thee I have earned.[23]

Methodist

You have given me a charge, O God, a mission and
a purpose: may You be glorified. I offer all that I am
and all that I have to do Your will. Empower me,
Gracious God, and prepare me to give an accounting
to You of my life as a servant to Your people. Help
me to watch and to pray and to rely only on You,
my calling to fulfill. In the name of Jesus, the
model of a faithful servant, I pray. Amen.[24]

Moravian

Gracious God, each moment of life is Your gift to us and we don't know what it will hold or what that moment will call us to do or be or face, yet we step out into it without choice, for who but You can hold back time. I ask that You constantly walk with me into this adventure. Sometimes that next moment is like climbing a mountain trail: placing one foot in front of the other repeatedly until the top is reached, but sometimes that next moment is looking for a handhold or a toe block on the way up a steep cliff! Without Your guiding Spirit I don't know where to put that toe or what to grab hold of: is it an anchored root I grab or a snake? Lead my life as You lead my ascent that I may be prepared for all the blessings You have in my future![25]

Native American

In harmony may I walk.
With harmony before me may I walk.
With harmony behind me may I walk.
With harmony above me may I walk.
With harmony underneath my feet may I walk.
With harmony all around me may I walk.
It is done in harmony.[26]

Pentecostal

Oh Lord, we believe life in this present age is
preparation for eternity. We joyfully look forward
to living with You forever. We anticipate a time
when all of the trials and tribulations of this
world will pass away, a time when there will be
no more sin, sickness, or sorrow. We will always
be happy and healthy. All will be holy. Hallelujah!
Our future hope helps keep us going even here
and now. In the midst of the difficulties and
problems of everyday life, we know in our hearts
Christ is coming and that He brings a better day.
Please help us then, Lord, prepare in advance lest
we miss the promise. Our eternal hope arises only

from our confidence in Your glorious grace. Yet we wish to so live and serve as to please our Lord and Savior. Direct us in the right path. Guide us in the good way. Reveal Your will. You created us for a special purpose. Your Son came into this world to seek and to save and to serve. He gave of Himself for others even unto death. Then the Spirit raised Him from the dead. Glory to God! Now Jesus is our example and model for all of life. Help us thus give of ourselves for others. Help us thus live and serve. Therefore, we strive not only to love God with our all, but we also strive to love every fellow human being by treating others as we want to be treated. As we boldly witness of Christ, we will do so in a way that respects those who follow other religions. Let us always remember that the true and living God is bigger and greater than any religious institution or human construction. Oh dear God, may we all come to know You better, deeper, truer! Amen.[27]

Presbyterian

Loving Lord God, in whom we live and move and have our being, we ask that You would help us to always be looking ahead. So that when our lives intersect with the lives of those in need, we will be ready to act. Give us an order to our lives that puts others before ourselves. Help us to seek the guidance of Your Spirit, to listen for Your voice, to trust Your hand, so that our will may become lost in Yours.

In Jesus' precious name we pray. Amen.[28]

Religious Society of Friends (Quaker)

O brother man, fold to thy heart thy brother:
Where pity dwells, the peace of God is there;
To worship rightly is to love each other,
Each smile a hymn, each kindly word a prayer.

For he whom Jesus loved has truly spoken:
The holier worship which He deigns to bless
Restores the lost and binds the spirit broken,
And feeds the widow and the fatherless.

Follow with reverent steps the great example
Of Him Whose holy work was doing good;
So shall the wide earth seem our Father's temple,
Each loving life a psalm of gratitude.

Then shall all shackles fall; the stormy clangor
Of wild war music o'er the earth shall cease;
Love shall tread out the baleful fire of anger,
And in its ashes plant the tree of peace.[29]

The Salvation Army

Loving God, I want to always be prepared in any
and every moment to be used by You. Take my
hands and use them to bless and help others. Take
my feet and guide my steps according to Your Holy
Word. Take my eyes and clarify my vision to see
people as You do. Take my ears and make them
keen to hear the voices of those who are forgotten,
ignored, and mistreated. Take my voice and fill my
mouth with words of kindness, encouragement,
and faith. Take my heart and let it be broken for
the poor, the outcast, the lost, the despairing, and
the wounded. Take my mind and grant me clear
thinking to recognize and value truth and goodness.

Take my will and mold it to Your purposes. Take my resources and help me to be a faithful steward of all the time, treasure, and talent You have entrusted to me.

I make this prayer in the name of my Lord and Savior, Jesus Christ.
Amen.[30]

Unity Churches

I fairly sizzle with zeal and enthusiasm and spring forth with a mighty faith to do the things that ought to be done by me.[31]

Zoroastrian

In humble adoration with hands outstretched
I pray to Thee, O God!
First of all,
through Thy Holy Spirit vouchsafe to me
All righteousness of action, all wisdom and
understanding, truth, and justice,
So that I may bring joy to all creation.
God is love, understanding, wisdom, and virtue.
Let us love one another;

Let us practice mercy and forgiveness;
Let us have peace, born of fellow feeling;
Let my joy be of altruistic living,
of doing good to others.
Happiness is unto him from whom happiness
proceeds to any other human being.

Truman's Prayer

Oh! Almighty and Everlasting God, Creator of
Heaven, Earth, and the Universe;
Help me to be, to think, to act what is right,
because it is right;
Make me truthful and honorable in all things;
Make me honest for the sake of right and honor and
without thought of reward to me.
Give me the ability to be charitable, forgiving, and
patient with everyone.
Help me to understand their intentions and their
shortcomings—even as You understand mine!
Amen.[32]

"An organization of this kind would fail in its object if it did not bring its members to a knowledge of religion. . . . If it were treated more as a manner of everyday life. . . it would not lose its dignity and it would gain a hold."[1]

—*Lord Robert S.S. Baden-Powell, 1908*

SCOUT PRAYERS AND DEVOTIONS

The development of a Scout's outlook begins with respect for God. On our journey along the Scouting trail there are many opportunities where we express thanks to our Creator for bringing us enjoyment, fellowship, and good health.

Since the founding of the Boy Scout movement there have been many wonderful prayers written and recited at meetings, outings, ceremonies, and other gatherings giving thanks and praise for God's blessings, guidance, and protection.

Included here is a short selection of traditional and popular Scouting prayers and devotions suitable for personal, group, and program use.

Cub Scouting

A Cub Scout Prayer I

Help us, dear God, to love You day by day,
To do our duty to You and enjoy our play.
To keep our Cub Scout Promise the best that we can,
And to do our best always to help our fellow man.

A Cub Scout Prayer II

Dear Lord,
Thank You for letting me be a Cub Scout.
Thank You for helping me to make new friends.
Thank You for my family who helps me.
Thank You for all the fun I have had.
And most of all,
Thank You for helping me when things are hard.

A Cub Scout Prayer III

O God, I do pray
For strength to live my best each day;
Draw near to me, and I shall see
The kind of Cub You'd have me be.

In serving others, I know it's true
That I am only serving You.
Fill me, dear God, with Your great love,
That I may be a better Cub.

A Pack or Den Prayer

We thank You, O Lord, for our pack (den); and
for all the boys and families who are touched by
Scouting. Make us strong as we work together to
help other people, and as we do our duty to You
and to our country. Help us remember to live by
the Cub Scout Promise and the Law of the Pack.

A Cub Scout Thanksgiving Blessing

Dear God, we ask for Your blessing
For loved ones and friends that are near.
We thank You for food and for love and for life
And the spirit of Cub Scouting that is here.
We thank You for leaders who care about boys,
Who give us their time—that's better than toys!
We thank You for parents who help us learn right,
For those who sew on our badges at night.
For all this, thank You dear Lord, up above,
For being a Cub is something we love!

Cub Scout Taps

Sun of Gold, Sky of Blue,
Both are gone from our sight, day is through.
Do your best, then to rest,
Peace to you.[2]

Cub Scout Vespers

As the night comes to this land,
On my promise I will stand.
I will help the pack to go,
As our pack helps me to grow.
Yes, I'll always give goodwill,
I'll follow my Akela still.
And before I stop to rest,
I will do my very best.[3]

Cubmaster's Benediction

May the Great Akela, leader of all Cub Scouts, guide
and guard our footsteps today, tomorrow, and for
all tomorrows to come.

CHAPTER FOUR: SCOUT PRAYERS AND DEVOTIONS

Boy Scouting

A Prayer for Scouts

O God of the mountain and valleys,
Of the forest, meadows, and plains.
Be our guide as we walk together the trail of life.
And may Your love, made known to us in the
stories of our faith,
Be known to others through the words and deeds
of our lives;
This day and always.

A Scout Prayer I

Dear God, help us to carry Your Spirit in our lives,
that we may share it with others by living it
ourselves.
Help us to offer all that we have and are in Your
service.
And help us to live the spirit of Scouting so Your
Spirit will live on through us.[4]

A Scout Prayer II

O Lord, we thank You for the work of Lord Robert Baden-Powell, who in his wisdom and vision founded the world Scouting movement.

We thank You for the efforts of those men and women who have brought Scouting to millions of youth the world over.

We dedicate ourselves to the principles of our Movement; To do our best to do our duty to God and our country.

We ask You, O Lord, to give us the strength and courage, each of us, to live up to the Scout Oath and Law, and the high ideals of the world brotherhood of Scouting.

A Scout Prayer III

Almighty God,
Help me to keep my honor bright,
And teach me that integrity of character is my most priceless possession.
Grant that I may do my best today,
And strive to do even better tomorrow.
Teach me that duty is a friend and not an enemy,
And help me face even the most disagreeable task cheerfully.

Give me the faith to understand my purpose and life,
Open my mind to the truth and fill my heart with
love.
I am thankful for all the blessings You have
bestowed upon my country.
Help me to know that a good nation must be made
from good people,
And to do my duty to keep it free.
Help me to remember my obligation to obey the
Scout Law,
And give me understanding, so that it is more than
mere words.
May I never tire of the joy of helping other people,
Or look the other way when someone is in need.
You have given me the gift of a body;
Make me wise enough to keep it healthy that I
might serve better.
You are the source of all wisdom;
Help me to have an alert mind,
Teach me to think,
And help me to learn discipline.
In all that I do and in every challenge I face,
Help me to know the difference between right
and wrong,
And lead me in obedience on a straight path to a
worthy goal.

Prayer for a Meeting

Dear Lord,
As we begin this meeting, we know that You are
here with us.
Make our hearts and minds ready to plan,
And do those things that will be pleasing to You;
And to serve our troop (patrol, crew, post, or ship),
our homes, our communities, and our country.
Where we fail, forgive us and help us start again in
the way You would have us go.

Boy Scout Oath Responsive Prayer

All: *On My Honor I Will Do My Best ...*

Leader: Almighty God, keep us always mindful
that our honor is a possession to be
cherished as dearly as life itself. Endow us
with firmness of purpose and uncommon
integrity that will enable us to fulfill
those responsibilities with which we are
charged. Make us ever conscious of the
trust others have placed in us as Scouts.

All: *To Do My Duty to God ...*

Leader: Creator of the universe, how often we
forget the true source of life's joys and

pleasures. How often, too, have we failed to remember the origin of the inward strength that has enabled us to be aware of Your continual presence in our daily lives. Help us to understand the rewards of service.

All: *And My Country...*

Leader: We thank You, Almighty God, for the privilege of living in the United States of America. Keep foremost in our minds that the freedoms that we enjoy were earned through the unselfish sacrifices of those who have gone before us. As the strength of a country is in her people, let us never avoid our responsibility to maintain this nation as a beacon of hope and freedom to all mankind.

All: *And to Obey the Scout Law...*

Leader: O God, accept the heartfelt thanks of us Scouts and Scouters for men of vision and leadership as Lord Robert Baden-Powell, Ernest Thompson Seton, Daniel Beard, and James E. West. Keep always before us the ideals that they set forth, and grant us the courage to live by them when others may not. Allow us never to forget that our actions may be the examples others choose to follow.

All: *To Help Other People at All Times...*

Leader: Grant us forgiveness, patient Lord, when we place the wants in our lives above the necessities of others. Teach us to recognize and understand the problems facing others and prepare us for each day's task of helping all those in need.

All: *To Keep Myself Physically Strong, Mentally Awake, and Morally Straight.*

Leader: God of our ancestors, let us never forget that our bodies and minds are but temporary gifts from You. Help us to preserve, strengthen, and use them for the betterment of ourselves, our homes, and our country.[5]

The Scout Law Prayer

Dear Lord, Bless all those everywhere who contribute to shape the hearts, minds, and bodies of Scouts. Let us remember what they have taught and apply it each day:

When facing deceit and dishonesty,
Let us be *Trustworthy*.

If we see stubbornness and unfaithfulness,
Let us be *Loyal*.
Where there is a disregard of others,
Let us be *Helpful*.
When we find people in despair,
Let us be *Friendly*.
In an atmosphere of bad manners,
Let us be *Courteous*.
Where there is cruelty and crudeness,
Let us be *Kind*.
Though wrongdoing and unruliness are common,
Let us be *Obedient*.
While others grumble and complain,
Let us be *Cheerful*.
In a world spoiled by waste and extravagance,
Let us be *Thrifty*.
When confronted with danger and temptation,
Let us be *Brave*.
As we see wickedness and unhealthiness everywhere,
Let us be *Clean*.
If we witness desecration and dishonor,
Let us remember to be *Reverent*.

As Scouts, let us stand out; our bodies strong, our
minds trained, and spirit true;
To You, Lord, our home and country we pledge
ourselves and our service.[6]

Scoutmaster's Benediction

The Scoutmaster's Benediction has its origins in Protestant church blessings given at the closing of worship services. The more familiar wording of this popular, one-sentence prayer first appeared in the 1927 book, The How Book of Scouting. *The next year, no less than three different versions were printed in the Boy Scout Service Library pamphlet,* Investiture Ceremonies, *beginning a tradition of its use to close meetings and other Scout functions.*

The following are five popular adaptations that have been often recited in one form or another since the early days of Scouting. These Scoutmaster Benedictions typically end with a customary "Amen," or "Goodnight Scouts," or "Goodnight Scouters," depending on context:

(And now) May the Great Scoutmaster of all good Scouts be with you (us) until we meet again.

May the Great Master of all Scouts be with us until we meet again.[7]

May the Great Scoutmaster of all good Scouts be between me and thee until we meet again.[8]

Let us pledge each other that we will keep Scouting friendships strong and deep until we meet again.[9]

⟶

May the Great Scoutmaster of all good Scouts watch us and guide us along the trail that leads to Him.[10]

Boy Scout Vespers

Softly falls the light of day,
As our campfire fades away.
Silently, each Scout should ask:
Have I done my daily task?
Have I kept my honor bright?
Can I guiltless sleep tonight?
Oh, have I done and have I dared
Everything to be prepared?

Quietly we join as one,
Thanking God for Scouting fun,
May we now go on our way.
Thankful for another day.
May we always love and share,
Living in peace beyond compare,
As Scouts, may we find
Friendships true with all mankind.
Quietly we now will part,

Pledging ever in our heart,
To strive to do our best each day
As we travel down life's way.
Happiness we'll try to give,
Trying a better life to live,
Till all the world
Be joined in love,
Living in peace under skies above.[11]

Leaders

A Leader's Prayer

Please God, grant me the spark to imagine,
The daring to innovate,
The discipline to plan,
The skill to do,
The will to achieve,
The commitment to be responsible,
And the leadership to motivate.

A Scout Leader's Prayer I

O Lord, we ask You for guidance in our daily task,
May virtue and leadership stand strongly among us;
To You we give all our thanks.

The Scout Oath, the Scout Law, their lessons
unfolding;
To our youth in numbers untold,
Our motto, our good turn, may we live and teach them.
Great Spirit of Scouting to You we pray.

A Scout Leader's Prayer II

O Lord,
Grant so that I may carry out in my life the spirit of
the Scout Oath and Law,
That I may teach it to others by living it myself.
Grant also that I may understand the true meaning
of service to others,
And humbly follow Your Spirit to be a worthy
example to my Scouts.[12]

A Boy Scout Leader's Prayer

Put me in touch with the heart of a boy,
Let me study his doubts and his fears.
Let me try to show him the way of life,
And help him avoid its tears.
For the heart of a boy in its buoyancy,
Is one that is pure and free;
So put me in touch with the heart of a boy,
The heart of the man to be.[13]

A Wood Badge Prayer

O God, take a Wood Badge walk with me,
And see what I've discovered;
An inner strength I hadn't known,
New skills that I've uncovered.

My body may feel tired now,
But my spirit soars on wings,
As I reflect on all we've done,
And heard, and felt, and seen.

Thank You for new friendships made,
And old bonds now renewed,
And help me live the Scout Oath and Law,
In all I say and do.

As I depart from Gilwell Field,
With ticket firm in hand,
Lord, help me do the best I can,
To help my fellow man.

For my journey does not end today.
In fact it is just the start.
So take a Wood Badge walk with me,
And hold me in Your heart.[14]

Wood Badge Benediction

And now in your journey, may the trail rise up to
meet your stride,
May the sun shine softly on your backpack,
May the cool, clean waters carry your canoe safely
to your next portage,
May the wind bring warm blessings to your
encampment,
May your Scouts find in you a fine example of the
adult they hope to be.
Peace be with you this day and forevermore.[15]

Outings and Activities

A Prayer for Travel or an Outing

Lord, protect and guide me as I set out this day.
Make my ways safe and my homecoming joyful.
Let me have Your wisdom so that I make good and
right choices in all the places that I go.
Give me enjoyable and steady companions and good
leaders, and let me not be lonesome.

A Prayer for Good Weather

Almighty and most merciful God, we humbly ask of You, in Your great goodness, to restrain any difficult conditions with which we will have to contend. Grant us fair skies.

Graciously hear us as Scouts who call upon You that, armed with Your light, we may travel without harm and cheerfully do our best in good fellowship.[16]

A Hiking Prayer

O God,
As we walk the majesty of Your creation,
We thank You for the open air,
For the sunshine and clouds,
For the early morning mist,
The noontime heat and the shadows of the night,
For the hills and the valleys,
The woods and the streams,
And all living things.
May Your Spirit be always with us as our constant companion,
And may the trail's end rise to greet us like the meeting of a friend.[17]

A Camp Prayer

Bless us, O Great Spirit, as Scouts gathered together
in this camp.
Grant that no harm may spoil our brotherhood.
Make us live together in wellness and good
fellowship,
Ever mindful of Your example and of our Scout
Oath and Law.
We thank You for old friends and for new
friendships.
We give thanks for the days of our gathering,
And we pray that we safely return to our homes,
With thanks for Your beautiful creation and the joy
of life.

A Prayer for Cheerful Service

O God, help us,
To do the work that lies before us this day,
Ably and cheerfully,
And in the spirit of glad sacrifice,
And bring us to our beds tired
But happy and healthy.[18]

A Fishing Prayer

Baden-Powell kept this well-known prayer on his desk at his English home, Pax Hill.

Lord, suffer me to catch a fish
So large that even I
In talking of it afterwards
Shall have no need to lie.

Graces and Other Blessings

Philmont Scout Ranch Grace

For food, for raiment,
For life, for opportunity,
For friendship and fellowship.
We thank Thee, O Lord.

Florida Sea Base Keys Blessing

Bless the creatures of the sea,
Bless this person I call me,
Bless the Keys You made so grand,
Bless the sun that warms the land,
Bless the fellowship we feel,
As we gather for this meal. Amen.[19]

Northern Tier Wilderness Base Grace

For food, for raiment,
For life and opportunity,
For sun and rain,
For water and portage trails,
For friendship and fellowship,
We thank Thee, O Lord.

Scout Prayer of Thanks

Dear God, we thank You today
For the adventure of Scouting,
For the unselfishness of parents and mentors,
For the patience of teachers,
And for the encouragement of friends.

Philmont Scout Ranch Prayer of Thanks

We thank You, O God, for this day,
For morning sun and evening star,
For flowering tress and flowing streams,
For life-giving rains and cooling breeze,
For the earth's patient turning,
The changing of the seasons,
The cycle of growth and decay, of life and death.
When our eyes behold the beauty and grandeur of
Your world,
We see the wisdom, power, and goodness of its
Creator.
We awake and behold! It's a great day.

The Founder's Blessing

Dear Lord, we thank You for the many blessings and much happiness that You have granted us.

For such blessings, deeds of thankfulness are, in Your sight, more acceptable than mere words of praise. Therefore shall we render our thanks by working in Your cause and by doing that which is the truest service to You.

To this end, O God, help us by developing in us less of care for self and more of care for others.

Strengthen in us that love that binds us each to all and all to You, that through our brotherhood of Scouts, which under Your good care has spread across the world, we may help to bring about the spirit of goodwill and peace between the nations.[20]

Other Prayers and Devotions

On Wings of Eagles

Adapted from a Bible passage, this inspiring prayer illustrates the ambition and spirit of those young men who strive and achieve the highest rank in Boy Scouting, Eagle Scout.

Dear God,
I know those who are young grow tired,
And that Scouts can grow exhausted.
But with trust in You shall I find my strength renewed.
I will rise on wings like eagles;
I will run and not get weary;
I will walk and not grow weak.[21]

Philmont Scout Ranch Prayer

Almighty God of hill and plain,
Over which we hike in sun and rain,
On mountain top and valley low,
Protect us Lord wherever we go.
And from our grateful hearts we'll raise
Glad hymns of thankfulness and praise.[22]

The Scout Beatitudes

Blessed are the Scouts who are taught to see beauty
in all things around them,
For their world will be a place of grace and wonder.

Blessed are the Scouts who are led with patience
and understanding,
For they will learn the strength of endurance and
the gift of tolerance.

Blessed are the Scouts who are provided a home
where family members dwell in harmony and close
communion,
For they shall become the peacemakers of the world.

Blessed are the Scouts who are taught the value and
power of truth,
For they shall search for knowledge and use it with
wisdom and discernment.

Blessed are the Scouts who are guided by those with
faith in a loving God,
For they will find Him early and will walk with
Him through life.

Blessed are the Scouts who are loved and know that
they are loved,
For they shall sow seeds of love in the world and
reap joy for themselves and others.[23]

A Scout Psalm

The Lord God is our Great Scoutmaster who
provides all our needs.
He lets us camp in forests tall and meadows green.
He leads us on trails besides waters deep and still,
brooks babbling, streams rushing, and rivers raging.
He restores our bodies, minds, and souls, even as
we observe the eagle soaring to greater heights
above.
He encourages the Eagle Scout in his upward climb.
He teaches Cub Scouts, Boy Scouts, Varsity Scouts,
and Venturers to live the Scout Oath and Law.
Even though the trails may lead through dark
valleys with towering mountains, we are courageous
because He leads us onward.
He continually blesses us with food for mind and
body.
Even when others dislike or distrust us, He blesses
us with the gifts of love and forgiveness.
Surely, His goodness and mercy will sustain us all
the days of our lives.
And, when we climb the final trail through the
awesome pass that leads to the Great Council fire,
we shall join those who traveled the trail before us
and joyfully live with Him forever![24]

More Benedictions and Closings

Taps

Day is done, gone the sun,
From the lakes, from the hills,
From the sky.
All is well, safely rest,
God is nigh.

Thanks and praise,
For our days, 'neath the sun,
'neath the stars, 'neath the sky.
As we go, this we know,
God is nigh.[25]

Philmont Scout Ranch Benediction

May God bless us and protect us;
May God show us favor and be gracious to us;
May God show us kindness and grant us peace.[26]

Scouting Benediction I

Wood and water . . . wind and tree,
Wisdom . . . strength . . . and courtesy,
Scouting's spirit go with thee.

Scouting Benediction II

Dear God, thank You for the opportunity to be here in Your creation. Give us the strength to endure, the wisdom to enjoy each moment, and the courage to push ourselves further than we have ever before. Bless our troop (patrol, crew, post, or ship) and our leaders as we journey through Scouting.

Scoutmaster's Responsive Benediction

Leader: And now, may the blessings of our Great Scoutmaster rest upon each of us and upon all Scouts and may we always follow the trail of honor and service.

Leader: A good Scout is prepared;
All: *We are prepared, Sir (Ma'am).*

Leader: A good Scout does at least one good turn daily;
All: *It has been done, Sir (Ma'am).*

Leader: Then I charge you to go forth for God, your country, your home, and your fellow Scouts.

Leader: Good night, Scouts!
All: *Good night, Sir (Ma'am).*

Prayer for the Centenary of Scouting

Loving God,
In this Centenary of Scouting,
We come before You as Your children.
We come to thank You.
To thank You for our founder, Baden-Powell,
for·his vision and his faith;
To thank You for the many leaders and volunteers
who have given their time, their energy,
and their commitment;
To the great game that is Scouting;
To thank You for all the children and young people
who have enjoyed and benefited so much from
Scouting through the past one hundred years.
And, loving God, we pray that You may be with us
through the next century.[27]

5

"God is . . . a vast Spirit of Love that overlooks
differences of form and creed and denomination and
which blesses every [person] who really tries to do
their best." [1]

—*Lord Robert S.S. Baden-Powell, 1930*

MY PERSONAL PRAYERS

These pages are for recording your personal and favorite prayers.

IN OUR OWN WAY

CHAPTER FIVE: MY PERSONAL PRAYERS

_____

_____

_____

_____

_____

_____

_____

_____

_____

_____

_____

_____

_____

_____

_____

_____

_____

_____

_____

_____

_____

_____

_____

_____

_____

_____

_____

_____

_____

_____

_____

_____

_____

_____

_____

_____

_____

_____

_____

_____

_____

_____

CHAPTER FIVE: MY PERSONAL PRAYERS

_____

_____

_____

_____

_____

_____

_____

_____

_____

_____

_____

_____

_____

_____

_____

_____

_____

_____

_____

_____

_____

_____

_____

_____

_____
_____
_____
_____
_____
_____
_____
_____
_____
_____
_____
_____
_____
_____
_____
_____
_____
_____
_____
_____
_____

CHAPTER FIVE: MY PERSONAL PRAYERS

_____

_____

_____

_____

_____

_____

_____

_____

_____

_____

_____

_____

_____

_____

_____

_____

_____

_____

_____

_____

_____

CHAPTER FIVE: MY PERSONAL PRAYERS

NOTES

Preface

i   From *The Aim of the Scout and Guide Movement*, London: The Boy Scout Association 1921, and *Scouting for Boys*, London: Horace Cox, 1908, 6 vols.

ii   From *Rovering to Success: A Guide for Young Manhood*, London: Herbert Jenkins, 1930.

Introduction

i   Estimation of prayer frequency based on "Faith-Based Funding Backed, but Church-State Doubts Abound: Section IV. Religion in American Life," from the Pew Research Center for the People & the *Press Survey Report,* April 2001.

ii   From *Aids to Scoutmastership: The Theory of Scouting for Scoutmasters*, by Baden-Powell, London: Herbert Jenkins, 1919.

Chapter One

1   From *Scouting for Boys* (see preface, n. *i*).
2   Written by Reverend Dr. Daryl B. Ingram.
3   St. Gregory of Nareg (10th century).
4   From 'Abdu'l-Bahá.
5   Written by Reverend Reginald T. Fletcher.

6   From Chapter 12, *Worthy Leader*, in the *Flower Adornment Sutra (Avatamsaka Sutra)*. English translation by the Buddhist Text Translation Society, Talmage, California.

7   St. Augustine of Hippo (354-430).

8   Written by Reverend Robert J. Thornton. The inspiration for this prayer comes from Psalm 8.

9   From *Science and Health with Key to the Scriptures*, 1875, pg. 16, by Mary Baker Eddy, founder of the Church of Christ, Scientist.

10   From the *Manual of The Mother Church*, pg. 41, written by Mary Baker Eddy. Praying (not just saying) this prayer each day is a duty for members of The Mother Church (the international church headquarters in Boston, Massachusetts).

11   Alma 37:35-37, the Book of Mormon. From the ancient prophet, Alma in 73 B.C.

12   Written by Richard Roper.

13   Written by Reverend Herbert F. Freitag.

14   Excerpt from a Scout prayer written by Wallace B. Smith.

15   The prayer "Heavenly King."

16   From the Book of Common Prayer.

17   Adapted from *Heaven and Hell* 22, by Emanuel Swedenborg.

18   "Tvamev Mata," a common Hindu prayer, origin unknown.

19   Quran 4:131.
20   This prayer is recited upon arising each day.
21   Written by Michael Reid Trice, Ph.D.
22   Extracted from a Christian prayer and adapted by Meher Baba.
23   Based on the poem, "O God, My Hope, My Heavenly Rest," by John Wesley.
24   Written by Reverend Franklin C. Jones.
25   Excerpt from *The Seven Sacred Prayers*, written by Elder Noel Knockwood of the Mi'kmaq (Micmac) tribe, the First Nations People of Nova Scotia.
26   Written by Dr. Tony Richie with assistance from the New Harvest Church midweek sanctuary class.
27   Daily prayer from the Book of Common Worship.
28   "Dear Lord and Father of Mankind" a hymn with words by John Greenleaf Whittier, an American Quaker poet (1807-1892). These words are from the long narrative poem, "The Brewing of Soma," written by Whittier and published in *Atlantic Monthly*, April 1872.
29   Written by Lieutenant Scott Hurula.
30   "Prayer for Protection" written by James Dillet Freeman (1912-2003), the Unity Church's Poet Laureate. This prayer was written during World War II and was taken on the first

manned moon landing in July 1969 by Apollo
11 astronaut and pilot, Edwin E. Aldrin Jr.

31 This version is from the Book of Common
Prayer.

Chapter Two

1 From *The Aim of the Scout and Guide Movement*
(see preface, n. *i*). Here Baden-Powell is quoting
Thomas Carlyle (1795-1881), a Victorian essayist
and historian.

2 Written by Reverend Dr. Daryl B. Ingram.

3 From the Matins Service of the Armenian
Church.

4 From 'Abdu'l-Bahá.

5 Written by Reverend Cassandra Carkuff
Williams, Ed.D., Th.M.

6 The thoughts of Vajra Banner Bodhisattva,
An Awakened Being, from Chapter 25, *Ten
Transferences*, in the *Flower Adornment Sutra*
(*Avatamsaka Sutra*). English translation by the
Buddhist Text Translation Society, Talmage,
California. Further noted is that a Buddhist's
character, strength, and courage come from
learning unselfishness.

7 St. Ignatius of Loyola (1491-1556).

8 Written by Reverend Robert J. Thornton.

9 Written by J. Houston Costolo.

10   Written by Reverend Herbert F. Freitag.

11   From "Dear Lord of Heaven and Earth,"
     written by Everett S. Graffeo.

12   From "Prayer for the Acceptance of God's
     Will," by Metropolitan Philaret.

13   "Prayer of Self-Dedication" from the Book of
     Common Prayer.

14   Adapted from *Divine Providence* 73, by
     Emanuel Swedenborg.

15   Bhagavad Gita (10:12), (7:7), (10.11).

16   This is a standard Muslim prayer that has been
     adopted over the centuries, and there is no
     known source.

17   Recited on festivals and high holidays.

18   Written by Michael Reid Trice, Ph.D.

19   From "Of Greater Worth Than Devotion,"
     written by Meher Baba, from *Treasures*, edited
     by Jane Barry Haynes.

20   Based on the poem, "One Thing with All My
     Soul's Desire," by John Wesley.

21   Written by Reverend Franklin C. Jones.

22   Translation into English attributed to Lakota
     Chief Yellow Lark, Indian missionary and
     medicine man, in 1887.

23   Written by Dr. Tony Richie with assistance
     from the New Harvest Church midweek
     sanctuary class.

24 Written by Adrian McMullen.

25 James Nayler, an early English Quaker leader (1618-1660).

26 Written by Lieutenant Scott Hurula.

27 "The Prayer of Faith," written by Hannah More Kohaus. This prayer-poem first appeared in *Wee Wisdom* in the early 1900s. *Wee Wisdom* was the longest-running children's magazine in publication.

28 Haptanghâiti: Yasna 35-2.

29 Reinhold Niebuhr, 1943.

Chapter Three

1 From *Aids to Scoutmastership* (see intro., n. *ii*).

2 Written by Reverend Dr. Daryl B. Ingram.

3 St. Neress the Grace-filled (12th century).

4 From Bahá'u'lláh.

5 Written by Reverend Reginald T. Fletcher.

6 From Chapter 40, *Universal Worthy's Practices and Vows*, in the *Flower Adornment Sutra* (*Avatamsaka Sutra*). English translation by the Buddhist Text Translation Society, Talmage, California.

7 St. Francis of Assisi (1181-1226).

8 Written by Reverend Robert J. Thornton.

9 "To Be Prepared," written by Brigadier General Norman Hoffman, USA, Retired.

10 Written by Reverend Herbert F. Freitag.

11 Written by Howard S. Sheehy, Jr.
12 From "Prayer at the Beginning of the Day" by Metropolitan Philaret.
13 From the Book of Common Prayer.
14 Adapted from *Apocalypse Explained* 1148:4, by Emanuel Swedenborg.
15 Taittiriya Upanishad 1:1.2.
16 Quran 2:250.
17 Ibid., 2:286.
18 Ibid.
19 Ibid., 7:89.
20 Ibid., 66:8.
21 Recited every Sabbath.
22 Written by Michael Reid Trice, Ph.D.
23 From "May Thy Will Be Done," by Meher Baba, October 1959.
24 Based on the poem, "A Charge to Keep I Have," by John Wesley.
25 Written by Reverend Franklin C. Jones.
26 Diné (Navajo) prayer, author unknown.
27 Written by Dr. Tony Richie with assistance from the New Harvest Church midweek sanctuary class.
28 Written by Adrian McMullen.
29 "O Brother Man, Fold to Thy Heart," a hymn with words by John Greenleaf Whittier (see chap. 1, n. 28).
30 Written by Lieutenant Scott Hurula.

31 This affirmation was written by the Unity Church's co-founder, Charles Fillmore.

32 An edited version of Harry S. Truman's favorite prayer that he used during many challenging times in his life. Truman was the 33rd president of the United States of America.

Chapter Four

1 From *Scouting for Boys* (see preface, n. *i*).

2 From *Scouting Magazine*, December 1966. Submitted by Mrs. Gordon H. Batten of Mountainside, New Jersey.

3 Usually sung to the tune, "Oh, Christmas Tree" ("O Tannenbaum").

4 From *A Memorial to a Scouter*, by Laird Vanni.

5 "On My Honor," an interfaith responsive reading written by Dr. Carroll Osburn, 1997.

6 The last two lines of this prayer adapted from the *Boy Scout Handbook*, 6th edition, 1963, pg. 439.

7 Courtesy of Ernie Doclar.

8 Attributed to Joel Ketonin. From a prayer printed in a Cumberland, Pennsylvania, Scout Show brochure in 1928.

9 From the second verse of the song "Till We Meet Again," published by the B.S.A. in *Round the Campfire*, 1958.

10 From *Investiture Ceremonies*, Boy Scouts of America Service Library, Series B, no. 3, 1928.

11 See chap. 4, n. 3.

12 Adapted from "Leadership: Prayer 92," in *Prayers for Use in the Brotherhood of Scouts*, 1927.

13 Source attributed to the Pictou County District Council, Nova Scotia.

14 From the poem "Take a Wood Badge Walk with Me," by Diane Miller.

15 Adapted from an old Gaelic blessing.

16 Adapted from a prayer written by Colonel James H. O'Neill, Chaplain of the Third Army, on orders from General George S. Patton Jr., December 1943.

17 Adapted from "For the Great Outdoors: Prayer 51," in *Prayers for Use in the Brotherhood of Scouts*, 1927, and the "Hiking Prayer," translated and adapted from French by Dr. Chau T. Phan, from Fernand Lelotte, S.J., *Rabboni: Consignes et prières pour mieux server, 9th Edition*, 1958.

18 Adapted from "A Prayer of Robert Louis Stevenson for Cheerful Work," in *Prayers for the Use in the Brotherhood of Scouts*.

19 Written by John Hammond.

20 Contemporary adaptation of a prayer written by Robert S. S. Baden-Powell as quoted in, *Baden-Powell: A Family Album*, written by his daughter, Heather Baden-Powell.

21 Adapted from Isaiah 40:30-31.

22 Usually sung to the tune of the United States "Navy Hymn."

23 Adapted from the Sermon on the Mount recorded in the Gospels of Matthew and Luke.

24 Adapted from Psalm 23.

25 These stanzas were written for a 24-note bugle call composed in July 1862 during the American Civil War by Union General Daniel Butterfield with Private Oliver Wilcox Norton. "Taps" became an official Army bugle call in 1874. Though there are many accepted versions, "Taps" has no formal or standard written verses.

26 Benediction used at Philmont Scout Ranch interfaith services.

27 Written by Father John Seddon, National Chaplain, England and Wales, for the 100th anniversary of World Scouting. National Catholic Scout Fellowship of the United Kingdom (with permission).

Chapter Five

1 Excerpt from *Rovering to Success* (see preface, n. *ii*).

SELECTED BIBLIOGRAPHY

Internet Resources

BeliefNet. *Beliefnet Home Page*, 2006,
        <www.beliefnet.com> (July 2006).

Hare, John Bruno. *Internet Sacred Text Archive*, 2006,
        <www.sacred-texts.com> (September 2006).

Hendra, Kyna. "The MacScouter's Big 'A Scout Is Reverent'
        Resource Book." *The MacScouter–Scouting
        Resources Online*, February 2001,
        <www.macscouter.com/ScoutsOwn> (July 2006).

Metzloff, Peter. "The Big Book of Scout Worship Services."
        U.S. Scouting Service Project, July 1999,
        <http://usscouts.org/usscouts/reverent.asp>
        (July 2006).

The Pluralism Project at Harvard University. *Pluralism
        Project Home Page*, 2007, <www.pluralism.org>
        (March 2007).

The World Prayers Project. *World Prayers Index*, 2005,
        <www.worldprayers.org> (August 2006).

SELECTED BIBLIOGRAPHY

Books

Appleton, George (General Editor). 1985. *The Oxford Book of Prayer*. Oxford: Oxford University Press.

Baden-Powell, Heather. 1986. *Baden-Powell: A Family Album*. New York: Hippocrene Books.

Boy Scouts Association. 1927. *Prayers for Use in the Brotherhood of Scouts*. Rochester: Kent, Great Britain: Stanhope Press.

Boy Scouts of America. 1928. *Investiture Ceremonies for Tenderfoot, Second Class and First Class Scouts and for Installation of a Troop*. Boy Scouts of America Service Library, Series B, No. 3.

Church Commission on Scouting (National). 1968. *When Scouts Worship*. St. Louis: Bethany Press.

Philmont Scout Ranch. 1994. *Eagles Soaring High: Trail Worship for Christians, Muslims, and Jews*. Boy Scouts of America, No. 5-877.

ACKNOWLEDGMENTS

I owe a debt of gratitude to my business associate,
David C. Scott, for his advice and collection of
historical documents and books that helped this
work become a worthwhile addition to the large
body of religious Scout literature. This project would
not have found a timely way to production without
the support of Stanley E. Allred and my other
business partners at Red Honor. Thanks go to Bob
Reitz, Curator of the Jack Harbin Scout Museum at
Camp Wisdom in Dallas, Texas, for his assistance
with historical Scoutmaster Benedictions and other
prayers. Ernie Doclar, Editor Emeritus of *Scouting
Magazine*, and Burts Kennedy, Associate Director of
Cub Scouting, Retired, for the National Office of the
Boy Scouts of America, gave helpful critical reviews
of Chapter Four to improve the selection and quality
of Scout prayers. I am grateful to Father John Seddon,
National Chaplain, England and Wales, for permission
to use his prayer honoring the 100th anniversary of
international Scouting. My thanks to Paul Moynihan,
Archivist, and Chris James, Head of Corporate
Communications, both of The Scout Association (U.K.),
in granting permission for the use of Baden-Powell's
early Boy Scout illustrations and quotations. A special

thanks to Susanna Daniel for making invaluable improvements to the readability and organization of the manuscript, and Alan Hebel and Ian Shimkoviak for their inspiring creativity in book design and layout that lifted the presentation of prayers beyond my expectations. My former National Scouting Museum colleagues and dear friends Lauré Cameron and Sarah Dunn gave helpful comments and suggested many creative ideas during the early stages of the book's development. I also thank Matthew Land and the staff at Publications Development Company for thoughtful and diligent editing, proofreading, and quality checking of the final manuscript and layout.

I searched an extensive collection of official, volunteer, nationally, and internationally produced books, publications, and other sources to find popular Scout-themed prayers and devotions for use in Chapter Four. In some instances, I edited prayers to make them consistent in context and voice, as well as more readable and relevant to the present American Scout program. But in no way was the original intent of a prayer altered. Every effort was made to connect the prayers to a deserving contributor. Wherever appropriate or when no names were obtainable a citation was given to the most recent Scout-themed worship or prayer resource available electronically or in print.

I am not qualified to speak for any religion, faith group, or denomination or to solely prepare an anthology of prayers from such a diverse set of beliefs. To avoid the obvious pitfalls, I had the rare pleasure of working with religious organizations, church leaders, and faith-based youth programs across the United States in compiling and arranging material for use in this book. Any anxiety I had concerning the collective participation of so many faith traditions for this project was quickly dispelled by the enthusiasm and support I received from everyone involved. In each instance and without hesitation, the purpose of the book was embraced. Every person and group dedicating their valuable time recognized the merits of including prayers in this unique context. I am deeply indebted to those individuals and institutions for their contributions of these special inspirational devotions that affirm the foundational ideals of the Scouting movement.

Those who graciously assisted me with this book in alphabetical order of their respective faith were:

African Methodist Episcopal
REVEREND DR. DARYL B. INGRAM
Secretary-Treasurer, Christian Education, African Methodist Episcopal Church, Nashville, Tennessee

ACKNOWLEDGMENTS

Armenian Apostolic

ELISE ANTREASSIAN
Coordinator of Christian Education, Department of Youth and Education, The Diocese of the Armenian Church of America (Eastern), New York, New York

Bahá'í

REGINA RAFRAF
Spiritual Assembly of the Bahá'ís of Dallas, Texas

ELLEN PRICE
Bahá'ís of the United States, Evanston, Illinois

Baptist

REVEREND REGINALD T. FLETCHER
National Coordinator for Youth and Campus Ministries, National Ministries, American Baptist Churches USA, Valley Forge, Pennsylvania

REVEREND CASSANDRA CARKUFF WILLIAMS, ED.D., TH.M.
National Coordinator, Discipleship Resource Development,
National Ministries, American Baptist Churches USA, Valley Forge, Pennsylvania

ACKNOWLEDGMENTS

Buddhist

REVEREND HENG SURE, PH.D.
Director, Berkeley Buddhist Monastery,
Berkeley, California
Buddhism representative to the Global Council
of the United Religions Initiative,
San Francisco, California
Member, Board of Directors, Interfaith Center at the
Presidio, San Francisco, California

Catholic

MONSIGNOR JAMES PATRICK MORONEY
Executive Director, Secretariat for the Liturgy,
United States Conference of Catholic Bishops,
Washington, D.C.

Christian Church (Disciples of Christ)

REVEREND ROBERT J. THORNTON
Disciples Home Mission of the Christian Church,
United Christian Church, Clayton, Ohio

Church of Christ, Scientist (Christian Science)

TMC YOUTH
The First Church of Christ, Scientist,
Boston, Massachusetts

ACKNOWLEDGMENTS

Church of Jesus Christ of Latter-day Saints (Mormon)

BRADLEY D. HARRIS
Associate Professor, Recreational Management
and Youth Leadership, Brigham Young University,
Provo, Utah

Churches of Christ

KENT BARNETT
Executive Director, Members of Churches of Christ
for Scouting, Abilene, Texas

**BRIGADIER GENERAL NORM HOFFMAN,
UNITED STATES ARMY, RETIRED**
Eugene, Oregon

J. HOUSTON COSTOLO
Elder, Picayune Church of Christ,
Picayune, Mississippi

RICHARD ROPER
Relationships Minister, Glenwood Church of Christ,
Glenwood Springs, Colorado

ACKNOWLEDGMENTS

Community Churches

REVEREND HERBERT FREITAG
President, International Council of Community
Churches, Chapel-By-The-Sea,
Clearwater Beach, Florida

REVEREND MICHAEL E. LIVINGSTON
President, 2006–2007, National Council of Churches
USA, New York, New York
Executive Director, International Council of
Community Churches, Frankfort, Illinois

Community of Christ

WALLACE B. SMITH
President Emeritus, Community of Christ,
Independence, Missouri

EVERETT S. GRAFFEO
General Officer, Community of Christ

HOWARD S. SHEEHY, JR.
Member of the First Presidency, Community of Christ

GAIL MENGEL
Ecumenical and Interfaith Officer, Community of Christ

Eastern Orthodox

GEORGE N. BOULUKOS
National Chairman, Eastern Orthodox Committee of Scouting, Freeport, New York

FATHER MICHAEL BRUCE JOHNSON, RETIRED
Pacific Northwest Outreach Coordinator, Eastern Orthodox Committee of Scouting,
Seattle, Washington

Episcopal

REVEREND DR. GWYNNE GUIBORD
Officer of Ecumenical and Interfaith Concerns, the Episcopal Diocese of Los Angeles, California
Consultant for Interfaith Relations, Office of Ecumenical and Interfaith Relations, the Episcopal Church, New York, New York

General Church of the New Jerusalem (The New Church)

REVEREND KURT HORIGAN ASPLUNDH, RETIRED
General Church of the New Jerusalem (The New Church), Bryn Athyn, Pennsylvania

ACKNOWLEDGMENTS

Bronwen Henry
Assistant Director of General Church Outreach,
General Church of the New Jerusalem

Hindu

Dr. Bhupendra Hajratwala
President, North American Hindu Association,
Pleasanton, California

Islamic

Daisy Khan
Executive Director, American Society for Muslim
Advancement, New York, New York

Jewish

Ari M. Gordon
Assistant U.S. Director of the Department of
Interreligious Affairs, The American Jewish
Committee, New York, New York

Rabbi Gary Greenebaum
U.S. Director of the Department for Interreligious
Affairs, The American Jewish Committee,
New York, New York

ACKNOWLEDGMENTS

BRENDA SHEA
Department for Interreligious Affairs, The American
Jewish Committee, New York, New York

Lutheran
MICHAEL REID TRICE, PH.D.
Director, Ecumenical Formation and Inter-Religious
Relations, Evangelical Lutheran Church in America,
Chicago, Illinois

Meher Baba
Committee for Meher Baba and Scouting, North
Myrtle Beach, South Carolina

Methodist
REVEREND W. DOUGLAS MILLS, PH.D.
Associate General Secretary for Dialogue and
Interfaith Relations, General Commission on
Christian Unity and Interreligious Concerns, the
United Methodist Church, New York, New York

Moravian Church
REVEREND FRANKLIN C. JONES, S.T.M.
Moravian Church Northern Province, Lake Auburn
Church, Victoria, Minnesota

ACKNOWLEDGMENTS

Native American

BEVERLY SMITH
Naakaii Diné/Kinlichiinii, Diné (Navajo) Nation,
Grandfalls, Arizona

Pentecostal

REVEREND DR. TONY RICHIE
Pentecostal representative in ecumenical and
interfaith dialogue and Member, Commission of
the Churches on International Affairs of the World
Council of Churches, Geneva, Switzerland
Liaison for the Society for Pentecostal Studies to the
Interfaith Relations Commission, National Council of
Churches USA, New York, New York
Senior Pastor, New Harvest Church of God,
Knoxville, Tennessee

Presbyterian

ADRIAN MCMULLEN
Program Assistant for Youth Ministries, Presbyterian
Church U.S.A., Louisville, Kentucky

TAMMY WIENS SORGE
Associate for Spiritual Formation, Presbyterian
Church U.S.A., Louisville, Kentucky

ACKNOWLEDGMENTS

Religious Society of Friends (Quaker)

BRUCE BIRCHARD
General Secretary, Friends General Conference
of the Religious Society of Friends,
Philadelphia, Pennsylvania

SYLVIA GRAVES
General Secretary, Friends United Meeting,
Richmond, Indiana

The Salvation Army

LIEUTENANT SCOTT HURULA
National Scouting Liaison Officer, The Salvation
Army, Oakbrook Terrace, Illinois

Unity Churches

BERNADETTE SWANSON, LUT
Curriculum Editor, Association of Unity Churches
International, Lees Summit, Missouri

Zoroastrian

LOVJI D. CAMA, PH.D.
Founding member and former President, the
Zoroastrian Association of Greater New York,
Suffern, New York

ACKNOWLEDGMENTS

TEMILYN MEHTA
National Coordinator, Zoroastrian Good Life
Program, the Zoroastrian Association of Greater
New York, Suffern, New York

VIRAF GHADIALLY
Coordinator, Zoroastrian Good Life Program, the
Zoroastrian Association of Greater New York,
Suffern, New York

I have given my best effort to ensure that this book is suitable for every Scout and a variety of Scouting program and group activities. The practice of prayer is founded in personal faith and religious tradition, whether it comes silently from the heart or is shared with family, a congregation, or any gathering of fellow believers. This editor apologizes if any of the prayers or devotions in this book appears inappropriate or incomplete to the reader. Any suggestions for changes or additions are gratefully welcomed. Please send comments and prayer submissions to be considered for future printings to:

ATTN: IOOW Book
Red Honor Press
P.O. Box 166677
Irving, Texas 75016

InOurOwnWayBook@redhonor.com

Robert Lee Edmonds has received numerous awards and recognitions for his contributions to science, industry, and education. Dr. Edmonds attended Loyola College, The Johns Hopkins University, and the Harvard Business School.

About Red Honor Press

Red Honor Press is a special imprint of
PenlandScott Publishers founded in 2006 for
the ambitious purpose of uniting timeless,
engaging, and enriching subjects and themes with
outstanding authors creating distinctive titles
for all ages and interests. Red Honor has quickly
emerged as a resourceful publisher of quality
educational, informative, inspirational books and
media. The Press also produces award-winning and
praiseworthy works for fraternal, faith-based, and
service-oriented groups and organizations. The Red
Honors mark of distinction—conceived by author
and naturalist Ernest Thompson Seton—reflects
the imagination and integrity underlying all Red
Honor Press publications.

The eagle feather and three circles of brotherhood
in the Red Honor Press colophon represent the
commitment of the company to the ideals
of Scouting and American values
in business and in life.